CONSTRUCTING
THE STABLE STATE

CONSTRUCTING
THE STABLE STATE
Goals for Intervention and Peacebuilding

KATHLEEN HILL HAWK

Westport, Connecticut
London

Library of Congress Cataloguing-in-Publication Data

Hawk, Kathleen Hill, 1963–
    Constructing the stable state : goals for intervention and peacebuilding /
Kathleen Hill Hawk.
        p. cm.
    Includes bibliographical references and index.
    ISBN 0–275–97755–2 (alk. paper)
        1. Humanitarian assistance—Case studies.   2. Humanitarian intervention—Case
    studies.   3. Peacekeeping forces—Case studies.   4. Political stability—Case studies.
    I. Title.
    HV544.5.H39   2002
    327.1'17—dc21   2002022471

British Library Cataloguing in Publication Data is available.

Library of Congress Catalog Card Number: 2002022471
ISBN: 0–275–97755–2

First published in 2002

Praeger Publishers, 88 Post Road West, Westport, CT 06881
An imprint of Greenwood Publishing Group, Inc.
www.praeger.com

Printed in the United States of America

The paper used in this book complies with the
Permanent Paper Standard issued by the National
Information Standards Organization (Z39.48–1984).

10 9 8 7 6 5 4 3 2 1

For Howard and Griffith Hawk,
Vance and Deanna Hill,
Don Snow, Allan Spitz,
and Roy Meek

Contents

Introduction

In recent years, increasing attention has been focused on the large number of people dying in the internal conflicts occurring around the world. As the news media have broadcast pictures worldwide of the casualties—up to 90 percent of whom are noncombatants—many citizens have clamored to their governments to "do something" to stop the violence. With the end of the cold war and the success of the concerted action to push Iraq out of Kuwait, there were high hopes that the United Nations could play an active role in saving "succeeding generations from the scourge of war" as expressed in the preamble of its charter.

In this context, external actors have intervened in a number of internal conflicts throughout the 1990s, generally justifying the action on humanitarian grounds. In most cases, external military intervention largely halted the fighting and allowed humanitarian assistance to be distributed. However, it has become painfully apparent to the international community that simply halting the fighting has not allowed these countries to create stable governments and harmonious societies. Thus, if intervention is to have any lasting impact, the external actors have recognized that it is necessary to undertake what increasingly is being called "post-conflict peacebuilding."

Post-conflict peacebuilding, as commonly used, refers to operations that begin after an end to the violence has been negotiated (or imposed) and attempt to bring about an environment that can create a stable, self-sustaining peace. Depending upon the needs of the society, this may include efforts to reform state institutions, promote economic development and ethnic tolerance, develop political parties, hold elections, foster civil society, and other projects.

It is difficult to say precisely how many peacebuilding missions have been undertaken in recent years. The United Nations Security Council does not specifically invoke that term in authorizing missions, which generally remain grouped under the term "peacekeeping." Since 1991, thirty-six new peacekeeping missions have been established, twenty-six of which have since been completed. While some (such as the mission to Ethiopia and Eritrea) perform the "traditional" peacekeeping tasks of observing an existing cease-fire or peace agreement and interposing a neutral force between international foes, most include additional tasks that to some degree fall within the newer designation of peacebuilding. Although the United Nations has been placed as the overseer in most formal peacebuilding missions to date, an end to the hostilities has often been brought about by a regional actor—sometimes with, sometimes without, a UN blessing. Interventions in Somalia, Haiti, Bosnia, Kosovo, and East Timor fall into this category.

In Somalia, the international community's first major attempt to reform a collapsed state in the post–cold war environment, the peacebuilding effort clearly failed—or more accurately, never got off the ground. In most of the other missions, it is less clear—and less useful—to categorize them simply as a success or failure. Elements of success can be seen, but they often coexist alongside serious shortcomings. Additionally, because the interventions have been undertaken within recent years, many missions are still under way.

This study is based on the premise that if external actors—foreign governments, international organizations, and private groups—cannot figure out how to lay a foundation for a longer-term stable peace, there will be decreasing support for international intervention and peacekeeping/peacebuilding missions in the future. If a military intervention is only able to accomplish a temporary respite in the violence that will resume once the external forces have been withdrawn, it becomes difficult to argue that its costs (in terms of lives and money) are worth the limited gains.

This study argues that, although the external actors have attempted to do many things in the aftermath of a military intervention toward consolidating peace, sufficient attention has not been paid to reconstructing the state as a capable, effective, and legitimate entity. Although reconstructing the state is only a portion of what needs to be done to bring about a stable, long-term peace, it provides a necessary foundation upon which to structure the other activities.

While theoretically neat but nearly impossible in practice, I have separated the concept of the state from that of the government. For purposes of this study, the state is essentially a framework of rules that structures and bounds the behavior of both the government and its citizens. The government is the group within a society that is delegated authority to manage its day-to-day affairs. Ideally, the government must act in accordance with the rules established by the state and can be held accountable for its actions. I argue based on the literature that a state must perform functions on three dimensions: First, the state must be *capable* of exercising authority over its territory and providing security to its citizens. Second, the state must be *effective* at resolving conflicts through its institutions and promoting the general welfare of its citizens. Third, the state must form a political identity and be viewed as *legitimate* by those who live under it. These three dimensions can be envisioned to form a three-legged stool. The state at once must be able to enforce its rules, resolve conflicts and promote the welfare of its citizens, and be accepted as legitimate. If one leg is weak, the others may compensate for it to an extent for some period of time. However, the structure is not viable over the long term if one leg is deficient or missing.

This does not mean that external actors should support an authoritarian government or help the strongest faction consolidate its power, although these might be the quickest solutions if all we seek is an end to the present violence. It does mean that if we desire to leave a stable (preferably democratic) country that is capable of sustaining peace, we need to do more than simply stop the fighting and conduct elections. We need to help (re)construct a state that is able to control its territory, assert its authority over those who may challenge it, and provide security to its citizens; a state that is able to mediate demands among groups within the country and design and implement policies to promote economic development and an improved quality of life; a state that is able to be a source of political identity for its citizens who deem it a legitimate entity to wield authority. It means that one cannot have a stable democracy without having a capable, effective, and legitimate state as a foundation.

However, none of this is to say that the state must be (re)constructed to resemble the centralized, autarkic state that developed in Europe in the eighteenth and nineteenth (and even early twentieth) centuries. New forms may be developed in which the state shares power, authority, and even sovereignty with institutions both below and above it. However, functions of authority and security, institutional and economic development, and identity based on legitimacy must be provided, either by traditional state institutions or by a hybrid design.

ORGANIZATION OF THE BOOK

To establish the rationale for defining a state on the three dimensions previously described, chapter 1 reviews the academic literature related to state development and discusses the concept of sovereignty and the impact of assaults on the state from above (globalization) and below (ethnic nationalism). Chapter 2 introduces the framework for the three case studies that comprise the heart of this study and explains the methodology used to explore them. Chapters 3, 4, and 5 cover the case studies of Somalia, Bosnia and Herzegovina, and Kosovo, respectively.

Chapter 6 then draws twenty-three lessons from the three case studies. Nine of these lessons are applicable to military intervention in general, while fourteen are specific to statebuilding efforts. Finally, chapter 7 presents a series of conclusions and recommendations for future attempts to bring a stable peace to a society in conflict.

CHAPTER 1

THE STATE OF THE STATE

This study argues that for peace to be secure over the longer term, a capable, effective, and legitimate state must be created in the wake of the internal conflict. However, before that case is made fully, it is important to understand what a state is and the justifications for defining it along the three dimensions cited.

WHAT IS A STATE?

In Europe to a much greater degree than in the United States, a distinction often is made between the *state* and the *government*. As it evolved in Europe, citizens were viewed as having a duty to serve the state, which was essentially a means for the monarchs to conduct their proclaimed "divine right" to rule. In this sense, the state was an extension of the ruler, or, as French King Louis XIV famously declared, "L'état c'est moi" ("I am the state"). Even after Western Europe became democratic, the notion of the state having interests separate and above the day-to-day political debate has continued to exist. While the roles of leaders vary, a distinction continues to be made in most European countries between the head of state (who by and large symbolizes the long-term interests of the country) and the head of government (who is the current political leader of the dominant party in the political system). In the United States, this is less pronounced, but is captured somewhat in the distinction between the *government* (in Europe, the state) and the current *administration* (in Europe, the government) in power (Steiner 1998). Viewed in this manner, the state could be considered an entity independent of the current government.

This distinction, in practice, is quite difficult to make. This is especially true in the less-institutionalized developing world, where the state apparatus is largely beholden to the current ruler. In many ways, however, this lack of distinction may be an important cause of the problems investigated in this study. If the group in power continually manipulates the state and its constitution—which essentially outlines the structure and organization of the government as well as the relationship between the powers of the government and the rights of its citizens—there is no covenant or mechanism to limit the government's behavior. Hence, people who occupy the bureaucratic positions become beholden to the ruler, not to the impartial rules embodied in the notion of the state.

For the purposes of this study, a state is viewed as a framework of rules and ideas that structures and bounds the behavior of both the government and citizens within a defined territory. In order to be able to do this, a state must be able to perform three tasks: (1) it must be capable of exercising its authority over its territory and providing security to its citizens, (2) it must be effective at resolving conflicts through its institutions and promoting the general welfare of its citizens, and (3) it must provide a political identity based on accepted legitimacy.

The State as an Authority to Control the Territory and Provide Security

Many of the most basic definitions of a state start from the premise that control over the defined piece of territory is a precondition for a state to accomplish anything else. While most writers take their definitions beyond simple control of territory, the notion that a state must wield a monopoly on the legitimate use of force often is the foundation upon which the other aspects are built. Thus, while control may not be sufficient for a state to accomplish its tasks, it can be considered a necessary condition.

Max Weber's ([1922] 1964, 156) treatment of a state often is used as the basis from which many scholars begin their discussions. He stated that the primary formal characteristics of the modern state are as follows:

It possesses an administrative and legal order subject to change by legislation, to which the organized corporate activity of the administrative staff, which is also regulated by legislation, is oriented. This system of order claims binding authority, not only over the members of the state, the citizens, most of whom have obtained membership by birth, but also to a very large extent, over all action taking place in the area of its jurisdiction. It is thus a compulsory association with a territorial basis. Furthermore, today, the use of force is regarded as legitimate only so far as it is either permitted by the state or prescribed by it. . . . The claim of the modern state to monopolize the use of force is as essential to it as its character of compulsory jurisdiction and of continuous organization.

Thus, for Weber, the state was essentially a compulsory association of rule by persons over other persons that rested on the use of legitimate force to compel those within the specified territory to obey the authority of those who ruled at any given time.

Thomas Hobbes ([1651] 1968) argued that centralized control over the means of violence was a prerequisite to security because enmity and distrust arise from the inevitable competition among men that ensues in the state of nature. Thus, citizens had to give absolute power to the government in order to protect themselves from other citizens. Hobbes reasoned that unless the state is able to provide protection, groups within the territory necessarily would resort to self-protection, and each man would be out to injure the other before he was injured himself. As Hobbes stated, in the absence of central authority, life was "nasty, brutish, and short." In keeping with Hobbes's prognosis, in current civil conflicts where the government is either unable or unwilling to provide security to its citizens, many groups find it necessary to defend themselves, generally by accumulating small arms and organizing into militias. However, this accumulation of weapons and organization gives that group an inherent offensive capability vis-à-vis other neighboring groups, who, in turn, feel compelled to arm and organize themselves in order to protect their members (Brown 1997; Posen 1993). Thus, a security dilemma is bred. John Herz (1950, 157) well explains the concept:

Whenever such anarchic society has existed—and it has existed in most periods of known history on some level—there has arisen what may be called the "security dilemma" of men, or groups, or their leaders. Groups or individuals living in such a constellation must be, and usually are, concerned about their security from being attacked, subjected, dominated or annihilated by other groups and individuals. Striving to attain security from such attack, they are driven to acquire more and more power in order to escape the power of others. This, in turn, renders the others more insecure and compels them to prepare for the worst.

In order to end an internal conflict, the security dilemma must be resolved and a central authority must be (re)constructed that is able to exercise authority over society. The state, not rival groups, must be vested with a monopoly on the legitimate use of force. The parties to the conflict must be confident that the national army and police forces, particularly if controlled by an opposing group, will not be used against them once they surrender their arms and disband (Steadman 1997; Walter 1997).

In addition to resolving the defensive incentives for acquiring power that may lead to conflict inherent in the security dilemma, offensive incentives for conflict must also be taken into account (Doyle and Sambanis 2000). Offensive incentives arise because factions and their leaders want to impose their ideology or culture on others, reap the spoils of state power, seize the property of rivals, exploit public resources for private gain, or any combination of these. Peace thus requires the elimination, management, or control of "spoilers" (Steadman 1997) or "war entrepreneurs" (DeFigueiredo and Weingast 1999).

As part of exercising authority over the territory, the state also must provide order and predictability to allow political, economic, and social development to occur—what scholars increasingly call the "rule of law." At a basic level, the rule of law establishes principles that constrain the power of the government, oblige it to conduct itself according to a series of prescribed and publicly known (or at least knowable) rules, and to ensure that people and groups are treated equally by the institutions administering the law (e.g., the courts, police, civil service) (Kritz 1996; Lipset 1994). This allows people and groups to predict with reasonable certainty the consequences of their actions (at least as far as the state is concerned). As a practical matter, the rule of law requires the government to respect the political and civil liberties granted to the citizens in the constitution and subordinates governmental power to legal authorities established by the state.

The State as an Administrative Unit

In addition to controlling the territory and providing security, a state also must provide for the other needs of society. This encompasses the necessity of organizing a system of governance and developing appropriate institutions to conduct that rule. It also necessitates the coordination and facilitation of the provision of services and collective goods that private individuals are unable (or unwilling) to provide for themselves.

States can be organized in many ways. An extensive body of literature exists that examines how different forms of political institutions can be used to manage conflict within divided societies (e.g., Lapidoth 1996; Lijphart 1977; Smooha and Hanf 1992; Steiner 1998). Institutions, broadly understood as a relatively stable collection of practices and rules defining appropriate behavior for specific groups of actors in specific situations (March and Olson 1998), serve to facilitate social interaction by reducing uncertainty regarding the regulation of human behavior (Levi 1990; North 1990; Przeworski 1991).

The institutional design of a state can be viewed as one means of regulating behavior and facilitating cooperation among groups. Federalism or autonomy arrangements may decrease the stakes of political competition by partitioning the exercise of power and allowing subnational groups to exercise a great deal of control over their own affairs. Although institutional arrangements can take different forms and involve different issues, the intent in regulating behavior is to provide conflicting groups with policymaking influence, autonomy, and a sense that they have a means of protecting themselves from the exercise of power at the center (Hartzell 1999; Lipset 1994).

To select persons for positions of power, pluralistic societies may utilize majoritarian, proportional, consociational, or corporatist methods. In divided societies, the latter three categories may guarantee that losing an election is not a matter of losing the means of protecting the survival of the group (Sisk 1996). Similar strategies can be used to guarantee minority members certain high-level positions in the government or by ensuring that the different groups are represented in the army, police force, and even general bureaucratic positions. For example, the 1999 Lomé Peace Accords tried to lay the basis for resolving the ongoing conflict in Sierra Leone by awarding four ministerial and four subministerial posts to the rebel Revolutionary United Front (RUF). While there were a number of weaknesses in this accord, it is an example of how governmental positions can be allocated to opposition groups so that they have the ability to protect their interests from within the system.

Development economists and policymakers have long recognized that the nature of official policies and state institutions does matter in efficiency and economic growth (Olson 1996). While many of these power-sharing institutional arrangements may enhance the legitimacy of the state, they usually come at some expense in efficiency and perhaps overall effectiveness, due to redundancies and the lack of qualified personnel in most war-torn societies. The concern most often raised is whether the enhanced legitimacy comes at the expense of more rapid economic development. Ottaway (1999) points out that the long-term support for a state may hinge on the success or failure of the economy, and rapid growth after a conflict, even if it is from recovery rather than true growth, is important.

A number of recent studies have also begun to examine a country's economic structure, especially the extreme dependence upon primary commodity exports, as being an impetus to conflict (Collier 2000; De Soysa 2000; Doyle and Sambanis 2000). The studies suggest that resource abundance and the revenue streams it generates affect the proper development and functioning of state institutions, fueling corruption and leading to perverse subsidization policies and budgetary mismanagement.

World Bank president James Wolfensohn has stated that there is no point in even talking about development strategies for countries whose governments are heavily involved in the theft of public monies (World Bank 1998). The difficulty in controlling corruption is that there are no internal structures in many countries capable of holding the government accountable for its actions. Although many external strategies to reduce corruption aim for a limited role of the state in society and a slimmer government bureaucracy, Reno (1998) cautioned that less government has contributed not to better government, but rather to "warlord" politics in the African countries he examined.

Reno argued that some internal warfare, and the rise of so-called warlords and other armed factions, developed out of a relationship between private power, commerce, and state institutions in weak states. He claimed that since rulers derived income independently from the enterprise of the country's population (from foreign government assistance and taxes on the export of natural resources), they preferred to conserve resources that otherwise would be spent for services, devoting them instead to paying off key strongmen in return for obedience and support. In this situation, a ruler may conclude that crippling the arms of the state is a rational action in an attempt to ensure that strong state institutions are not co-opted by a rival.

The practical outcome of this situation is that some rulers abjure broader national interests in favor of enriching themselves and co-opting or seeking to destroy others who may threaten the system. They neither have, nor seek, the legitimacy of the citizens of the country. For their part, the citizens suffer neglect and the ravages of conflict while the state provides them with little or no benefits in terms of economic development, education, or health care. Those opposed to the government are forced to resort to violent tactics, as no institutions exist that are capable of resolving opposition within the system (Dahl 1966).

The State as a Political Identity Based on Legitimacy

Few scholars believe that modern states can be based on pure power and control alone. Even if it desired to, a state cannot station troops outside of everyone's home to enforce its rule. The alternative is the accepted domination of state power based on a shared political identity, rooted in legitimacy.

Early notions that the state had to be deemed "legitimate" in the eyes of its subjects began to be seen during the late 1600s and into the 1700s in Europe in the writings of John Locke and Jean Jacques Rousseau, among others. Locke ([1689] 1980) argued that it was the duty of government to protect citizens' rights to life, liberty, and estate, and if the government did not do this, citizens had the right to revolt. Rousseau ([1762] 1997) saw the purpose of the state as "the preservation and prosperity of its members," and if the state overplayed its control functions, it would lose the willing allegiance and legitimizing support of its population.

In his work, *Economy and Society*, Weber ([1922] 1968) claimed that continued domination had to legitimize itself in one of three ways. First, he set forth that domination could be founded on rational rules that are based on obedience to norms, not a person. He saw this form as being structured by the means of a bureaucracy, which rested on the regular and continuous fulfillment of official duties with rules restricting the use of coercion. Weber viewed a bureaucracy as an efficient means for transforming social desires into rationally organized action because it contained objective, calculable rules, and therefore was superior to other forms of collective behavior.

The second form of domination discussed by Weber was that of personal authority based on tradition. The patrimonial structure that necessarily arose was based not on obedience to impersonal purpose and abstract norms as in the bureaucratic structure, but strictly on personal loyalty. It lacked the bureaucratic separation of the "private" and the "official" sphere. The political power of the ruler was part of his personal property, and his exercise of power was discretionary. An official's loyalty was to his relationship with the ruler, not to his impersonal tasks. Weber saw patrimonialism as accumulating wealth not by exchange, but by taxation, and lacking the procedural and political predictability that was necessary for the development of capitalism.

Charisma, Weber's third form of domination, was based on qualities of a specific person who enjoyed loyalty and authority by virtue of a mission believed to be embodied in him. While bureaucracy and patrimonialism were rooted in satisfying the everyday—especially economic—needs of citizens, charismatic domination often arose out of the anxiety and enthusiasm of an extraordinary event (heroism). By nature, charismatic domination was not a continuous institution, but one that gained and retained power by proving the leader's power in practice. However, as soon as charismatic domination lost its personal foundation (e.g., the leader dies) and its emotional faith, Weber pointed out that its allegiance with tradition was the most obvious and often the only alternative. Its structure had to be routinized to allow the newly privileged social and economic strata to preserve their positions in a depersonalized form.

The notion that people should feel an attachment to their state is a relatively recent phenomenon. Up until the late eighteenth century, the determination of a "state" was not based on national sentiment, identity, or consciousness, but on the ability of the leader to defend its territorial boundaries (Linz and Stepan 1996). The ruler of a state could transfer people and territory almost at will, without concern that the people had any attachment with one particular state or any right to dispute the actions of the state's leader. The concept that people could group themselves into a "nation"—what Weber ([1922] 1968, 11: 921–26) viewed as a "sentiment of solidarity in the face of other groups"—really only became an issue in the latter half of the nineteenth and early twentieth centuries (Conner 1990; Hobsbawm 1983). After the world wars, nationalism posed problems as countries sought to redraw boundaries, and the notion of self-determination was heralded as a desirable goal. While the dominant peoples in these new states may have felt liberated, minorities often felt repressed as the characteristics of the dominant groups became intertwined with new state institutions and imposed upon others who, if they protested, were accused of not being loyal to the state (Linz and Stepan 1996).

While many see nationalism as a necessary political identity, there is considerable dispute over the basis of the sentiment. While some see political identity as being based on ancient group relations (Huntington 1993; Kaplan 1994; Kissinger 1999; West 1941), others see it as a political construct, not a natural state of affairs (Gellner 1983; Hobsbawm 1993; Tyrrell 1996). Gellner parallels the rise of nationalism with the rise of industrialization, and claims that the governments have sought to create an integrated, homogeneous society needed by industry. Tyrrell suggests a symbiotic relationship between the state and nationalism, and claims that the enduring appeal of nationalism is based on a deeper psychological desire to be part of a group and to further the interests of their group—especially one based on less escapable features such as racial and national characteristics—rather than primordial ethnic ties. In this sense, nationalism can be seen as a consequence of the transition from traditional agrarian societies to modern, industrial ones in that nationalism becomes a means of self-identification and fosters a sense of belonging in the alienating, impersonal modern world.

It is useful to distinguish between what may be termed exclusive (or ethnic) nationalism and inclusive (or civic) nationalism (Greenfeld 1997; Snow 1996). Exclusive nationalism tends to draw support from citizens who share certain inherent characteristics, such as race or religion. This form of nationalism can degenerate into a "we" versus "they" mentality, and, in the extreme, justify such actions as genocide and ethnic cleansing. Inclusive or civic nationalism, on the other hand, is something that one can choose—or choose not—to support that leads citizens to rally around a common center.

Much recent attention has been drawn to the concept of civil society, an aspect of civic nationalism, and the role it plays in stabilizing societies. Two versions of the civil society argument can be found in the literature. In the first version, civil society comprises an independent sphere of action, capable of energizing resistance to the state. The Solidarity movement in Poland in the 1980s is an example of this form (Foley and Edwards 1996). The second version, symbolized by Putnam's (1995) concept of "social capital," focuses on networks, norms, and social trust that facilitate coordination and cooperation for mutual societal benefit. In his study of state governments in Italy, Putnam (1993) found that although all of the regional governments seemed identical on paper, their levels of effectiveness varied dramatically. He claimed that the quality of governance was determined by long-standing traditions of civic engagement (or its absence), and that the states in northern Italy did not become civic because they were rich, but became rich because they were civic.

THE EVOLUTION OF STATES

According to the above definition, a well-functioning modern state: (1) has a framework of rules that structures society and is capable of exercising authority over its territory and providing security to its citizens, (2) is able to resolve conflicts effectively through its institutions and promote the general welfare of its citizens, and (3) serves as a political identity based on accepted legitimacy.

Some have looked to Europe (especially northwestern Europe) as the model of how states develop (accepting the principle that all states essentially must pass through a series of similar stages and will eventually come out of the process resembling the Western European states of today). However, it is important to realize that not all states were created "equal" and that they have evolved—and will evolve—differently depending on the unique features of their histories, geographies, cultures, and the numerous other factors that shape their development. A closer examination of the areas experiencing many of the conflicts over the past decade suggests that external actors cannot just "push" many of the current societies in conflict along the path of state development. In many cases, a state must be constructed that is able to perform the functions identified as necessary in this chapter if a stable peace is to be sustained after an intervention. A brief summary of state development in Europe, the Balkans, and sub-Saharan Africa highlights some of these differences.

State Development in Europe

Ironically, some of Europe's good fortune may lie in the collapse of the Roman Empire and the weakness and division that ensued. Because Europe was not centralized, there was no single focus (or center of gravity) to capture, and the numerous marauding bands (Vikings, Russians, Moors, Magyars, and Turks, among others) were worn down, forced out, or incorporated (Landes 1999).

From about 1000 to the mid-1400s, Europe experienced a long period of population and economic growth—interrupted by the Black Death that claimed somewhere between a third and a half of the people in western Europe in the mid-1300s—as the continent became subject to fewer invaders from the outside. As population densities increased, European nations began to compete for territory. Tilly (1990, 54) noted that one of the main reasons for the creation of relatively centralized state apparatuses in Europe was the "continuous aggressive competition for trade and territory among changing states of unequal size, which made war a driving force in European history." In order to protect its citizens and prevent territory from being lost, the state had to link outlying areas to the center and place agents at territory edges. As the feudal system decayed, competition favored good care of subjects because people could leave one domain and move to another. Rulers had to bargain with citizens for taxes, military service, and cooperation in state programs. The growth of states in Europe was correlated with the development of urban areas, and the existence of intensive rural-urban trade provided an opportunity for rulers to collect revenues through customs and excise taxes, allowing the monarchs to bypass great landlords as they extended royal power to towns and villages (Tilly 1990). In order to attract labor to the cities, leaders had to bestow political and social rights on residents. Innovation generally was initiated from below, especially from the mercantile (business) communities in those cities, because they were allowed to reap the rewards in the market.

Additionally, the earliest modern states of Western Europe essentially were able to complete their statemaking process in three near distinct phases

(Tilly 1975). First, they established a centralized, "absolutist" state at the expense of a feudal order that had begun to lose much of its economic and political utility. Second, leaders welded together the subjects of the centralized monarchy into a people with a common history, legal system, language, and, quite often, religion (in the sense of Christian schisms), thus leading to the evolution of a national identity and the transformation of the centralized monarchical state into a nation-state. And third, the state gradually extended representative institutions (dictated by the necessity to co-opt into the power structure new and powerful social forces that emerged as a result of the Reformation, Enlightenment, and the industrial revolution) over a period of decades if not centuries.

Through a state-building process that took place over a period of three to five hundred years—during which time there was a tremendous amount of death, suffering, loss of rights, and unwilling surrender of land, goods, and labor—Europe was able to transform itself into the modern sovereign states of today (Tilly 1975). Additionally, Europe was able to develop sovereign states (defined as holding a monopoly of coercive power over their citizens and having an institutionalized administrative structure) a couple of centuries before the emergence of nationalism in the late 1800s and early 1900s (Ayoob 1996).

State Development in the Balkans

Although western (especially northwestern) Europe was able to evolve into reasonably coherent states between the sixteenth and nineteenth centuries, southeastern Europe was ruled by a series of multinational empires that spanned two millennia and only broke down in the late nineteenth and early twentieth centuries. Although medieval feudal kingdoms essentially existed within the empires, pre-modern state formation was short-circuited by absorption into the Ottoman Empire in the fourteenth century (Hagen 1999). Although the region that would eventually comprise Yugoslavia was largely inhabited by Slavic peoples, the Ottomans organized society more on the basis of religion than "national" identity, and new cleavages developed between the Catholic Croats, Muslim Bosnians, and Orthodox Serbs (Jelavich and Jelavich 1963).

As states were formed in the late nineteenth century as Ottoman rule receded, each state found that its territory only covered a portion of the areas inhabited by the "titular" national group and that substantial minorities were included within its borders. For example, Serbia did not encompass all of the areas in which Serbs lived, but did include a number of Croat, Bosnian, Albanian, and Hungarian settlements. As such, the Balkan states were all borne in the nineteenth and twentieth centuries as irredentist nations—each committed to the recovery of their "unredeemed" national territories. With their medieval dynasties and nobilities stripped of them by the Ottomans centuries earlier, the legitimacy of those who sought to lead the new Balkan states rested on their ability to embody the national "imagined community" (Hagen 1999). In the largely peasant societies, capitalist individualism possessed little prestige or legitimacy. Building armies capable of wresting away the unredeemed lands of the nation from their enemy possessors was the highest public value and the main duty of the state. However, a small tax base hindered the states, many of which sought loans from other countries, leading them to become pawns in the struggle among Europe's larger powers.

Beset by Balkan wars in 1912 and 1913, Europe became mired in the region's struggles with the assassination of Austrian Archduke Ferdinand in Bosnia (then a part of the Austro-Hungarian Empire) by a Serb terrorist, triggering the series of demands that would precipitate the First World War. At the conclusion of the war, faced with the revolutionary idea of a nation-state—that a national group and the boundaries of the state should coincide—the region's diversity became an acute problem.

State Development in Sub-Saharan Africa

Political geography has posed a completely different set of political challenges to state builders in Africa than it did to the Europeans. In a comprehensive study, Jeffrey Herbst (2000) argues that the fundamental problem facing state builders in Africa—be they pre-colonial kings, colonial governors, or presidents in the independent era—has been how to project authority over inhospitable territories that contain relatively low population densities.

Herbst (2000) argues that power in pre-colonial polities was not in the first instance based on control of land as it was in Europe where, due to population densities, it was in short supply. In pre-colonial Africa, the primary object of warfare—which was continual in many places—was to capture people and treasure, not land, which was available to all. Since few improvements were made to the land, it was often easier to flee stronger powers than to fight. Thus, the consequential role that war played in European state development in linking the hinterlands to the center was not replicated in Africa.

Central governments were often not concerned about what transpired in the outlying areas as long as tribute was paid and there were no imminent security threats emerging to challenge the center. In this sense, pre-colonial African states therefore had precisely the opposite physiology of many in Europe: the power assets were concentrated in the center with gradations of authority extending into the hinterland (Herbst 2000). With this context, pre-colonial political units in Africa were continually in flux, as areas would break off from the center whenever circumstances were favorable. Instead of pretending that a state controlled an area that it could not physically dominate, more nuanced notions of shared sovereignty were developed.

In many ways, the colonial system totally transformed the historical political geography of Africa in a few years' time and continues to cast its shadow today (Young 2000). Politically, colonialism imposed a hard system of boundaries, destroying the old political systems and undermining the traditional system of checks and balances. The boundaries drawn in European foreign ministries (for the convenience of the Europeans) did not take into account the realities on the ground, tying together numerous groups who shared no common language or culture and many times dividing ethnic groups among several colonial powers. In addition, the authoritarian method of rule relied heavily on coercion and frequently employed divide-and-rule tactics, further exacerbating ethnic tensions. The Africans themselves frequently copied these techniques after independence.

The colonial system in Africa profoundly reordered economic as well as political space (Young 2000). In exchange for the sacrifice of supplying governance services to foster trade and investment linkages—the "White man's burden" to civilize the natives—many Europeans felt entitled to exclusive economic benefits from the colonies. Restricting trade from the colony to the mother country, the Europeans (with the possible exception of Great Britain) tied the African territories to the metropolitan economies as subordinated appendages, often destroying intracolonial trade and regional trade in the process. In order to enhance their profits, the colonizers often forced the colonies to focus on a single cash crop or mineral. However, this process often destroyed the food production base, leaving the colony vulnerable to famines and swings in the international market. Territorial infrastructures, particularly transport and communications systems, were shaped by the vision of imperial integration and usually led directly to the port, allowing little, if any, internal interchange.

Colonial subjugation in Africa brought not only political oppression and economic exploitation, but also psychological humiliation as the colonizers imposed their religions, languages, and cultural practices upon African society. African culture was, for the most part, regarded as having little value, and its religious aspects—outside the zones in which Islam was well implanted—was subject to uprooting through intensive Christian evangelical efforts (Young 2000).

After World War II, world opinion turned against colonialism and a number of factors led to the rapid decolonization of much of Africa. The economic and political costs of managing the colonies were too high for European economies devastated by war. Most African colonies drew more from European treasuries than they brought in, and the notion that colonies brought countries strength and respect in the international arena was abandoned. As independence/nationalist movements within the colonies increased in strength, war-weary populations in Europe resisted calls to send their troops to quell the growing riots in the colonies.

African independence took place at a speed few predicted. Starting in northern Africa in the early 1950s, most of the continent became independent between 1956 and 1965. With the movement happening so rapidly, little attention was given to the viability of the newly independent entities, and the colonizers used their limited influence to further their own interests, not those of the Africans (Herbst 2000).

While much of the earlier stages of independence occurred peacefully—with the exceptions of Algeria and Kenya in the 1950s and early 1960s—the colonies often were left with little preparation and training in self-governance. Although there may have been some organization in some independence movements, once the colonial power left, groups within the countries often found little else to agree upon and power struggles developed, leading to weak, unstable governments.

Robert Jackson (1992) claimed that the acceptance of these new states in Africa by the United Nations signaled a movement from "empirical statehood" to a "rights-based" model. The 1960 UN General Assembly Declaration on the Granting of Independence to Colonial Countries and Peoples (Resolution 1514) called for the recognition of African states essentially because they deserved it as a result of the colonial experience, rather than by having to prove sovereignty by showing the establishment of a national government that could enforce authority over its territory.

Africa's new leaders quickly decided that the colonial boundaries should be retained and the "state" would remain as their system of organization, rejecting any return to the pre-colonial tradition of multiple sovereignties and soft boundaries. At the 1963 conference founding the Organization of African Unity (OAU) held in Addis Ababa, Ethiopia, the new leaders, while espousing rhetoric to promote pan-African unity, made a pact to retain the borders drawn by the colonizers and promised to refrain from interfering in the affairs of other states. The new leaders had a profound interest in maintaining the nation-states and boundaries they inherited from the Europeans because there was no guarantee, if they began to experiment with different types of political organization, that they would continue to be in power (Herbst 1996). Additionally, by reducing external threats to their power, they ensured themselves maximum flexibility to assert authority over their own populations.

With the international borders guaranteed by juridical sovereignty, and the major powers and dominant international organizations (such as the UN and the OAU) refusing to recognize secessionist movements, the rulers of the African states were not in danger of losing their territory if they failed to control it. And because the African states emerged during the cold war, the leaders were able to obtain financial and military resources from the two superpowers whose national security interests overrode concerns about the domestic policies and internal legitimacy of African leaders. This allowed the latter to secure revenue and weapons from external sources, bypassing the need to extract taxes and labor from their citizenry. In this manner, external actions played a major role in shaping the internal configurations of African states (Jackson 1992; Reno 2000b). Indeed, the possession of globally recognized sovereignty (with its access to assistance from international organizations and foreign governments) allowed rulers to claim resources from powerful outside patrons, enabling them to co-opt or suppress rival claimants to power. Government, in this sense, could become a protection racket run by the ruling elites for their own benefit, rather than a facilitating mechanism to meet the needs of society (Jackson 1992).

Although many have expressed hope that with the end of the cold war African states might be forced to improve domestic governance and develop internal legitimacy, multinational companies have stepped in and cut deals with many of the governments of these states, allowing their rulers to continue to eschew the needs of the broader population (Reno 1998). The international community does not seem to be interested in dealing with the contradictions in the notion of juridical statehood and control within a country's borders, and Africa suffers from neglect as the major powers generally focus on other regions deemed more important (Jackson 1992).

NOTIONS OF SOVEREIGNTY

The concept of sovereignty—the idea that the ruler of the state has ultimate legal authority with his country—is also important to the discussion of the role external actors can play in constructing a state in war-torn societies. Some argue that sovereignty, for the most part, precludes external intervention unless requested by the country's leadership. However, in recent years, as issues of government-sponsored ethnic cleansing and internal anarchy have come to the fore, others have argued that sovereignty, while providing rulers with certain rights, has its limitations and also should be viewed as carrying with it responsibilities for the well-being of the population (Annan 1999; Deng 2000). In his 1991 annual report, then UN Secretary General Javier Perez de Cuellar (1991, 13) stated that "[i]t is now increasingly felt that the principle of non-interference with the essential domestic jurisdiction of States cannot be regarded as a protective barrier behind which human rights could be massively or systematically violated with impunity." The argument is now being made that true sovereignty should be viewed as being held by the citizens of a country and only rulers that are freely chosen by those citizens can legitimately act as sovereign on their behalf (Deng 2000).

While the concept of sovereignty was first elaborated in the sixteenth and seventeenth centuries (notably by Jean Bodin and Thomas Hobbes), early formulations were written during periods of internal conflict and based upon the premise that unless the sovereign had supreme authority there would be no domestic order and justice. Although many credit the 1648 Peace of Westphalia for applying the principle to international affairs (largely due to the provision that princes could determine the religion within their own territories), the norms that comprise sovereignty in the nation-state system were not developed until much later (Krasner 2001).

Although the principle of sovereignty—and its companion principle of nonintervention—are reasonably well-institutionalized in the international system (in that they are embedded in most charters of international organizations), leaders throughout history have chosen to accept or ignore another country's sovereignty, depending on their level of power and their national—and even personal—interests. Sovereignty, in this sense, was a right that could only be exercised if one had the power to prevent others from encroaching upon it.

Part of the difficulty in dealing with the issue of sovereignty is that it means different things to different people in different contexts. In order to better understand the concept of sovereignty and the implications of international intervention, Krasner (1999) makes a useful distinction among four different usages of the term: international legal sovereignty, Westphalian sovereignty, domestic sovereignty, and interdependence sovereignty.

International legal sovereignty—or what Jackson (1992) and Jackson and Rosberg (1982) term juridical sovereignty—refers to the practices associated with mutual recognition, usually between territorial entities that have formal juridical independence. In this form, a state recognizes no higher authority than itself, so that in the anarchical international system, states are theoretically equal in the same way that individuals are equal at the national level. Almost all rulers have claimed international legal sovereignty because it provides them material and normative resources, enhancing their ability to stay in power and—if they so desire—to promote the security, economic, and ideational interests of their constituents. Different criteria have been applied regarding when a government deserves recognition as leading a state (e.g., Communist China versus the Nationalist Chinese government on Taiwan, or Slovenia's and Croatia's announced secession from the former Yugoslavia), but none has been consistent, and recognition is in many ways a political decision, rather than one conforming to a legal norm.

The second form, Westphalian sovereignty, refers to political organization based on the exclusion of external actors from authority structures within a given territory. The fundamental norm of Westphalian sovereignty is that states exist in specific territories within which domestic political authorities are the sole arbiters of legitimate behavior. As a right with no guarantees of the power to ensure it, Westphalian sovereignty is violated when external actors influence or determine domestic authority structures, whether coerced through external intervention or through voluntary invitation. For instance, Bosnia's Westphalian sovereignty—but not international legal sovereignty—has been compromised since independence, first by Serbia and Croatia, and then by international attempts to construct a multiethnic domestic authority structure.

Domestic sovereignty refers to the formal organization of political authority within the state and the ability of public authorities to exercise effective control within the borders of their own polity. As we see in Africa today, Somalia can have extremely limited domestic sovereignty without compromising its international legal or Westphalian sovereignty. The primary issues discussed in this study—such as whether a state is capable of exercising physical control over its territory, is able to effectively resolve conflicts and promote the citizens' welfare, and possesses legitimacy—are all factors that fall within the realm of domestic sovereignty.

Finally, interdependence sovereignty refers to the ability of public authorities to regulate the flow of information, ideas, goods, people, pollutants, or capital across the borders of the state. While it has become commonplace to note that state sovereignty is being eroded by globalization, such analysis is concerned fundamentally with questions of control, not authority. While a loss of interdependence sovereignty does not necessarily imply anything about domestic sovereignty, understood as the organization of authoritative decision making, it does undermine domestic sovereignty that is comprehended simply as control. In the developed world, the loss of interdependence sovereignty has led rulers to choose willingly to compromise their Westphalian sovereignty through international organizations like the European Union. In the developing world, the inability of a state to regulate the weapons and refugees that cross its borders has compounded its internal problems.

These distinctions are useful when one looks at international intervention for the purpose of constructing the state. International intervention inevitably affects some aspects of a country's sovereignty, but may leave others untouched. Thus, the issue of sovereignty precluding international intervention is less clear than many make it out to be.

International interventions generally do not affect the international legal sovereignty of countries. However, in cases such as Kosovo where an area seeks to secede from a state, intervention can profoundly alter it. In almost every instance of international intervention, Westphalian sovereignty is compromised because the intervention is intended to reshape the behavior of the target country. How long and to what degree Westphalian sovereignty is compromised depends largely on the goal of the intervention and whether one power simply is being displaced (as in the 1983 U.S. intervention in Grenada) or whether the outside power is intent upon reshaping society and creating new norms of cooperation and competition. Although domestic authority structures have been developed in Bosnia and are in the process of being developed in Kosovo, full Westphalian sovereignty has not been returned to either since an international administrator still has veto power over domestic decisions.

In the cases in this study, actions by governmental leaders who, through conscious action (in the Balkans) or incapacity (in Somalia), generally triggered the external intervention which set for itself the goal of transforming the domestic sovereign authority into a more capable and legitimate entity. In addition to more effectively organizing domestic authority, the intervener also has had to deal with refugees, with the transfer of weapons across borders, with drug trafficking, and with money laundering, all concerns related to interdependence sovereignty.

THE STATE OF THE STATE TODAY

In 1959, John Herz claimed that the nation-state was on its way out because its borders were no longer impermeable and it was unable to protect its citizens in the traditional manner. Although Herz (1968) later backed off on his claim, many scholars in recent years have returned to the question of whether the territorial state, as we have known it, will survive. Although centralized political units have existed throughout several millennia, the state has only served as the dominant organizing principle of the international system for the past three or four hundred years.

Numerous scholars have focused recently on assaults on the state by the twin pressures of globalization and ethnic nationalism (e.g., Barber 1992; Cerny 1995; Gaddis 1994; Hoffman 1998; Nye 2000). Their general argument is that globalization has led to a homogenization and integration of peoples across borders, weakening the state from above, while ethnic nationalism has led to creating subnational and ethnic borders, weakening the state from within. Thus, if states are being challenged from both above and below, it is important to examine whether it is feasible—or even desirable—to construct a state in the traditional manner.

The Globalization Challenge to the State

Transnational forces on the state are not new and, in many ways, states are more capable of dealing with them today than they were in the past (Krasner 2001). The printing press and the Great Depression ravaged societies to a much greater extent than have the Internet or the Asian flu. However, in today's globalizing system, the export and import of capital; the shifting of hundreds of billions of dollars around the world each day; and the decisions over investment and employment, wages, and production are all made primarily by private forces under little or no state control. In this context, globalization is changing the shape of state control and the basic rules of politics and international relations by altering payoff structures (Cerny 1995; Krasner 2001).

In this globalizing world, states are not simply losing autonomy, they increasingly are sharing powers with—and being pushed around by—businesses, international organizations, and nongovernmental organizations (Matthews 1997). While this diffusion of power away from the state may mean some issues can be dealt with more quickly, it also may lead to less problem solving, both within states and among them. It also may mean the provision of fewer international public goods, as there is no overarching entity (such as a national government within a country) to provide them.

While some may talk as if globalization were limited to the advanced industrialized world, it also has a pervasive effect on the developing world. Undoubtedly, globalization has brought information, ideas, and technologies to the developing world that has allowed it, in many ways, to "leapfrog" ahead. Advances in agricultural methods and the introduction of communications equipment (such as the cell phone and Internet) have allowed countries to technically advance more rapidly than through reliance on internally developed methods. The global media and nongovernmental organizations (NGOs) have made it harder for leaders to oppress citizens and blatantly manipulate the electoral process. Citizens in the developed world have called on their governments to take action in ending the massive starvation and human rights abuses in the developing world out of a concern for the plight of the affected people. Arguments are advanced that the integrating and homogenizing influences of market forces and information will mitigate conflict through increased interchange and awareness of other peoples with the hope that these will weaken exclusive loyalties and hasten the emergence of a world society.

However, globalization has not been without its negative aspects, such as allowing leaders to continue to forego developing ties with their citizens in favor of arrangements with international companies, offshore banking facilities, and foreign governments (Duffield 2000; Reno 1998, 2000b). Liberian warlord (now President) Charles Taylor is thought to have supplied, among other things, a third of France's tropical hardwood requirements through French companies (Reno 1996). During the latter part of the 1990s, the contribution of the rebel Union for the Total Independence of Angola (UNITA) movement to the ferocious war in Angola was largely underwritten by De Beers' no-questions diamond-buying policy and an unwillingness of many Western governments to uphold UN trade sanctions (Global Witness 1998).[1]

As long as the leader is able to control the commodity in demand, being able to assert authority over a fixed territory and to project power through traditional institutions are often not necessary. Instead of spending resources on "unnecessary" institutions, leaders use profits gained from contracts with international partners to co-opt or repress rivals. Campaigns of intimidation and violent population displacement often are not unfortunate and indirect consequences of conflict, but instead are its intended outcomes.

Although globalization has not caused this instability, it has facilitated the parallel and transborder economic linkages necessary for them to thrive and survive. Charles Taylor is estimated to have pocketed between $400 million to $450 million per year from the conflict in Liberia (Reno 1996). UNITA rebel leaders in Angola are estimated to have accumulated $3.7 billion in revenue between 1992 and 1998 (Global Witness 1998).

Assaults on the State from Within

If globalization is thought to encroach upon the state from above, then internal conflicts based on ethnic nationalism and greed can be said to encroach from within. In contrast to the earlier insurgencies that often appeared in countries that had achieved some level of modernization, the new conflicts generally occur in the poorest countries, with the fewest prospects of development, and often in what has been termed "failing" or "failed" states. In most cases, the violence is not the cause of the failing, but rather its result (Snow 1997).

Just as transnational threats to the state are not new, neither is ethnic nationalism. Two things have changed recently, however. First, there has been a decline in the level of external assistance directed to the national government, weakening its capacity to repress rival groups. Second, foreign countries are less willing to look the other way when a state attempts to brutally repress its citizens, especially if those citizens are of a minority ethnic group. Thus, with the end of the cold war, corrupt, patronage-ridden, ineffective governments are finding themselves increasingly challenged by different groups—often organized along ethnic lines—who were able to be dominated in the past and are now attempting to assert their autonomy (or even independence) from the state.

While nationalism was once largely a force for integration, today it is more often a reactionary, divisive force (Barber 1992). Wars fought in the name of nationalism are not instruments of policy, but often emblems of identity, expressions of community, and ends in and of themselves. The ethnic criteria by which groups define themselves may include common descent, shared historical experiences, and valued cultural traits. However, because such groups draw their strength from their cultural bonds, not associational ones, they cannot be treated as the equivalent of a political party or explained away by arguing that what "really" motivates such groups is the quest for power or well-being (Gurr 1996).

Many scholars argue that a person's political identity is socially constructed and malleable, not an innate feature (Gellner 1983; Greenfeld 1997; Gurr 1996; Hobsbawm 1990). Until forced to make a choice, many prefer to have multiple and complementary identities. However, when systematically repressed, inflamed, and/or manipulated by self-promoting leaders brandishing a cause, one identity often is forced to the forefront to unify a group around that bond to the exclusion of others. In creating a "we" versus "them" mentality, these ethnic groups tend to demonize and dehumanize "them" and often feel threatened and become aggressive—both to preempt perceived threats of malicious intent or aggression towards them and because of the perceived evil nature of the adversary (Greenfeld 1997). Victimization—whether real or imagined—often plays a role as well.

As is evident in the case of Kosovo, the manipulation of historical events is often fundamental to the creation of national movements (Mertus 1999; Renan [1882] 1996). But whatever the true history and the true roots of the conflict, once atrocities have been committed on the basis of ethnic criteria, the result is usually an ethnically polarized society (Ottaway 1999).

Another aspect of the challenge to the state from within is what Collier (2000) has claimed are greed-motivated rebellions. If, during the cold war, most internal conflicts still followed Carl von Clausewitz's famous dictum that war was a continuation of politics by other means, much warfare in the post–cold war era—especially when chains of command are weak—may be economics by other means (Duffield 2000; Keen 2000; Reno 1998). While many of these wars may have started with the aim of taking over the state (or of breaking away from it), many now appear to have mutated into wars where immediate economic agendas assume an increasingly important role (De Soysa 2000; Keen 2000).

While the extent to which grievances play a role in these newer conflicts is debated, grievance-oriented rebellions face massive collective action problems that greed-motivated ones do not (Collier 2000; Olson 1965). For example, there is no "free-rider" problem (where everyone, regardless of whether they participate in the rebellion or not, receives equal benefits) for greed-motivated rebellions because the benefits of the rebellion can be confined to those who participate in it. There is no coordination problem because the rebellion does not need to be so large as to be victorious nationally in order to profit. Additionally, there is no time-consistency problem because if rebellions are able to skim off some of the profits from primary commodity exports during the rebellion, then rebel recruits can be rewarded during the conflict rather than being dependent upon promises of future reward.

What increasingly is a cause for concern is that these new internal conflicts—whether related to either ethnic nationalism or greed—lack the traditional purposes of violence. With no clear political ideologies or objectives to guide or limit conflict and with no real "center of gravity" to sway or protect, these new internal conflicts are similar to international war, where groups do not necessarily seek to gain the support of the population, but rather to force the people out of the territory or destroy them (Snow 1997). Since there are generally no overarching political or military hierarchies, it is difficult to negotiate or to implement cease-fires with the ad hoc militias who frequently commit high levels of atrocities against the civilian populations and are able to secure resources that would be unavailable to them in times of peace. Up to 90 percent of the people who die as a result of these conflicts are civilians (Snow 2000).

Although abuses against civilians are usually portrayed as an unfortunate deviation from the laws of war or as a means to a military end, Keen (2000) argues that the "point" of these newer wars may lie precisely in the legitimacy they confer on these abuses, which in peacetime would be punishable as crimes. He says that whereas analysts have tended to assume that war is the "end" and abuses the "means," it is important to consider the opposite possibility: that the "end" is to engage in abuses or crimes that bring immediate rewards, whereas the "means" is the perpetuation of war. Thus, the common notion that war is a contest between two sides, with each trying to win, may be misleading in many newer internal conflicts. Seen in this light, warfare may be better viewed as the creation of an alternative system of power, profit, and protection than as a breakdown or collapse of the system. War, in this vein, may be advantageous for a number of groups within a society who therefore seek to perpetuate rather than end the violence (Duffield 2000; Keen 2000).

While many contemporary civil wars have been labeled as senseless, one can argue that, in some ways, nineteenth- and twentieth-century notions of interstate warfare were more senseless. When war is seen as an occasion for risking death in the name of the state (and with little prospect of financial gain), it may take months of brainwashing and ritual humiliation to convince new recruits of the notion. However, a war where one avoids battles, picks on unarmed civilians, and makes money may make more sense (Keen 2000).

The Future of the State

While it is apparent that the role of the territorial state as we have known it over the last 350 years or so is evolving, it is not clear toward what end. While the developed world has moved toward larger economic units through entities such as the European Union and trade blocs such as the North American Free Trade Agreement (NAFTA), many in the developing world are beset by calls for increased autonomy from minority groups and even outright secession in some areas. While not exclusionary, four potential futures are briefly presented below.

The most radical proposal for resolving many of these conflicts in the developing world is to reconstruct the state system so that the territorial boundaries correspond more closely to the social and cultural boundaries among people. However, many fear this approach would likely cause as many problems as it would solve (e.g., who would define which groups are able to become a state) and would create a host of difficulties on a practical level (e.g., forced population transfers). Africa alone has more than one thousand ethnic groups. Gurr (1993) contends that a more constructive approach would be to recognize and strengthen communal groups within the existing state system. In order for this to occur, he argues that the international community (through the threat of sanctions) must accept a common obligation to protect the collective rights of groups within such a system, including the right of expression without fear of political repression and the obligation of the dominant group not to impose its cultural standards or political agendas on others. Although many scholars think that some states may need to break up because they are too large in scale and/or too removed from local problems, there is also a general recognition that the idea of the nation-state—that the state's borders should be contiguous with those of a nation—is not feasible in the international system (Gurr 1993; Linz and Stepan 1996; Tilly 1992).

Benjamin Barber (1992), maintaining that neither "McWorld" (his synonym for globalization) or "Jihad" (his synonym for ethnic nationalism) wants or needs democracy, suggests that the most attractive democratic ideal in the future would be a confederal union of semi-autonomous communities smaller than nation-states, tied together into regional economic associations and markets larger than nation-states. He claims this would allow the entity to be participatory and self-determining at the bottom and representative and accountable at the top. In this scenario, the nation-state would play a diminished role.

James Rosenau (1990) suggests that a multi-centric system (actors with autonomous, transnational identities) now coexists with the state-centric system. He sees this as a compromise, rather than a rejection of the state-as-most-important-actor argument. He claims states still do—and will—wield most instruments of coercive power, although the range of issues on which they can be used has narrowed. Rosenau views the late twentieth century as a period of "cascading interdependence" based on rapidly changing patterns of interaction. He claims that the state's weakening authority has diminished it as the focal point for theory building, which may lead to role conflicts and the breakdown of previous understandings that held the international system together.

Nye (2000) claims that, contrary to many predictions, the state is not likely to become obsolete. He claims that people want three things from their political institutions: physical security, economic well-being, and a communal identity (all captured within the three dimensions of the state outlined earlier in this chapter), and that although changes in international processes slowly are shifting the locus of these values, the state has provided more of all three to its citizens than has any other institution.

While these four futures are not exhaustive of the directions in which the state system may evolve, they highlight the fact that the current system is not fully meeting the needs of states in the present day. Because a sharp break with the past is unlikely, the current state system will almost certainly be with us for many years to come as newer organizing principles gradually take hold over decades, if not centuries, just as the feudal system slowly gave way to the anarchical state system. The challenge, then, is not to simply reconstruct states according to what has worked in the past, but to recognize that newer conceptions may be found. While those conceptions will inevitably be grounded in the state system, creative ways to deal with both the challenges from above and below should be explored.

SUMMARY

In viewing a state as a framework of rules and ideas that structures and bounds the behavior of both the government and the citizens within a defined territory, one can see the state as a depersonalized instrument that is charged with fulfilling three basic functions of society. First, the state must be capable of exercising authority over its territory and regulating society so that it protects citizens' personal security and provides them with a foundation for the rule of law. Second, the state must be able to effectively resolve conflicts through its institutions and promote the general welfare of its citizens. Third, the state must become a source of political identity for the citizens based on the accepted legitimacy of its rule.

While these functions may sound basic to someone in the developed world, it is apparent that many states around the world are unable to fulfill them. While some argue that sovereignty precludes external action targeted to shape the internal behavior of states, external actors increasingly are attempting to prevent widespread harm to a country's citizens—whether it is from their own government's direct abuse or from other threats.

Globalization and internal conflicts have each impinged on the role of the state in recent years. While each provides significant challenges to the authority and control of the state over its territory, few see a viable alternative that is likely to replace the state as the locus of political organization in the near future. However, it is clear that the system is evolving, and most recognize that what has worked in the past may not hold all the answers in the future.

NOTE

1. De Beers and the World Diamond Council, a leading industry group, have since changed their policies and have been leading advocates of developing a system to police the rogue diamond trade in an attempt to disassociate themselves from the "blood diamonds."

CHAPTER 2

INTRODUCTION TO THE CASE STUDIES

In recent years, Somalia, Bosnia, and Kosovo have each experienced a violent internal conflict that prompted a foreign military intervention, largely because of humanitarian concerns and fear that the conflict would spread. Each case showed aspects of ethnic/clan warfare and of political leaders manipulating the conflicts for personal gain. In Somalia, the military aspects of the intervention were largely conducted by the troops under UN command. The five-month, U.S.-led Unified Task Force (UNITAF) mission in 1992–1993 is a notable exception to this, but that mission was limited to the provision of security for humanitarian efforts and did not seek to bring about a longer-term resolution of the conflict. In the Balkan cases, the intervention forces were under NATO command. While the United Nations eventually took upon itself the mandate to rehabilitate the political institutions and economy of Somalia, external actors went in with a comprehensive plan to do so in both Bosnia and Kosovo.

The effort in Somalia, which began in 1992, was the first intervention of this sort and, in many ways, shaped future humanitarian interventions. The major efforts in Bosnia occurred prior to those in Kosovo. I seek to understand if the later interventions were able to incorporate lessons learned from the earlier experiences and to examine how those lessons could—and should—be applied to future external actor decisions and strategies to intervene in a country in conflict. Since external actors have inserted troops into the internal conflict, they presumably had/have a vested interest in seeing that a stable peace is developed and domestic governance (re)constructed that can effectively resolve future problems before they again lead to an humanitarian emergency. The problem at the heart of this study is that while U.S.-led and NATO forces have been able to quell violence, the underlying problems in each country remain. The general expectation is that if the foreign forces were to leave Bosnia and Kosovo today, the territories would revert to anarchy and violence as happened previously in Somalia.

These countries have experienced large-scale, violent internal conflicts because the "state" is not capable of exercising its authority and providing security to its citizens, is not able to resolve the conflict through its institutions or to promote the general welfare of its citizens, and is not viewed as being legitimate by many of those who live under it.

The basic question addressed in these case studies is this: Did the external intervention conduct activities that would help that country develop a capable, effective, and legitimate state? To conduct these studies, I follow Alexander George's (1979) controlled comparison research strategy. For each case, there will be three sections: background, implementation, and an evaluation of the external intervention. The background section, examines a brief history of the country, the roots of the conflict, and how and why the conflict developed into a humanitarian problem that prompted international action. The implementation section outlines goals of the external actors drawing on the formal resolutions/agreements authorizing action and on public statements made by decision makers. The third section evaluates how well the external actions helped reconstruct the state. In this section—the heart of the comparison—two questions are examined. First, I ask whether the external intervention was successful in diffusing the humanitarian emergency in the short term. This is essentially a summary judgment of whether the external effort stopped the large-scale violence in the country and allowed the basic needs of the population to be met. At most, this might provide an opening within which the underlying issues could be addressed and political negotiations could take place—if the domestic parties so desired.

The second question looks at the longer-term effectiveness of the intervention and asks how well the external efforts have laid the foundation for a capable, effective, and legitimate state that can sustain peace in the future. In this sense, something that generally was not specified as an intended outcome of the external intervention is being evaluated. Therefore, I really am not looking to say whether the external effort succeeded or failed according to standards the international actors may (or may not) have set for themselves, but to look at what was done and attempt to ascertain whether the dimensions considered essential to "statebuilding" were addressed.

The overarching question raised in each case is whether or not an agreement has been signed to end the conflict. Signing a treaty has proven to be highly correlated with an end to the violence, whereas less formal agreements tend to break down more easily (Doyle and Sambanis 2000). While it is beyond the scope of this book to discuss how the international community can achieve this, a treaty generally provides an agreed upon structure of the state (or recognizes one from an earlier constitution). This "blueprint" is as important to statebuilders as one is to homebuilders. The plan to (re)construct a state must be set out in advance or the various elements of the structure are likely to lack the coordination and support necessary to sustain themselves in the wake of inevitable challenges, leading to the collapse of the process. If major issues are left unresolved, a firm foundation cannot be laid. However, it must be recognized that all agreements are not created equal, and the external actors must ensure that any agreement resolves the most important issues underlying the conflict in a manner that is sustainable and that provides the foundation for a capable, effective, and legitimate state.

Under the dimension of the state as an authority to control and provide security, the following three questions are examined:

Has the fighting ended and does the state have control of the territory?

At times, an agreement may precede the end of the fighting. At others, an end to the fighting (generally through a cease-fire) may precede the agreement. Whatever the case, it is impossible to begin the process of statebuilding until general hostilities have ceased. Authority cannot be established, security cannot be ensured, institutions cannot be developed, economic development cannot occur, and reconciliation cannot be brought about until large-scale fighting has ended.

Have the combatants been disarmed and demobilized?

In order to create a secure environment for peace, the armies and militias of the former combatants must be reduced, neutralized, and, if appropriate, professionalized and integrated into a national force (Hartzell 1999; United Nations 1996). Although it is a difficult and costly task (as money and often employment must be provided to the former combatants), a large number of men equipped with weaponry and no source of livelihood is a constant threat to the peace process as well as to the personal security of the citizens (Ottaway 1999).

Have the basic structures of the rule of law been (re)established?

Generally, this involves implementing a policing and court system capable of preventing small-scale violence between the formerly warring parties and ensuring the personal safety of returning refugees, displaced persons, and the general citizen population (Bair and Dziedzic 1998; Ball 1996; Plunkett 1998). Additionally, because large-scale internal conflicts generally lead to a breakdown of the criminal justice system and an upsurge in criminality, economic activity will be slow if the security of property and possessions is lacking (Collier 2000).

Under the dimension of the state as an administrative entity charged with resolving conflicts and improving the lives of its citizens, the following three broad questions are examined:

Have refugees been repatriated and internally displaced people returned to their homes?

The countries in this study each experienced massive population movements both internally and across borders. Much of the political, economic, and social reconstruction and reconciliation necessary to provide the foundation for a stable peace cannot begin to take place until refugees and displaced persons have returned to their homes. These returnees also provide much of the "glue" to hold multiethnic societies together (USIP 2000c). Additionally, until these people are reestablished, they are a destabilizing factor in the region and a burden on the international community.

Have political authority and institutions been (re)established in a manner that allows the citizens of the country to hold them accountable for their actions?

As James Madison noted in *The Federalist Papers* ([1788] 1987, No. 51, 356) some 230 years ago, "[i]n framing a government which is to be administered by men over men, the great difficulty lies in this; you must first enable the government to control the governed; and in the next place oblige it to control itself." Although political authority and institutions can be provided through many different forms of government, as a practical matter, the Western countries that will form the core of almost any statebuilding operation will not (re)construct a state on any other basis than according to democratic principles. While democracy can take a number of forms, it is at heart an accountability mechanism, allowing citizens (directly or indirectly) to participate in the selection of, and to exercise restraint over, their government. The challenge for external actors is to empower those who seek peace and democracy within the society and to design a system that rewards moderation and encourages compromise among contending interests (Paris 1997; Rothchild 1996; United Nations 1996).

Is economic development underway?

Many argue that economic development is a necessary precondition to resolving a large number of the problems underlying current internal conflicts (Ottaway 1999; Steil and Woodward 1999; USIP 2000a). If long-term stability is to be achieved—and nationalist politics to be avoided—people must develop a vested interest in peace and envision a future in which they can foresee an improving standard of living. In the context of a declining or stagnated national "pie," disputes often lead to a "we" versus "them" attitude that fuels ethnic or clan rivalries.

Under the dimension of the state as a source of political identity based on legitimacy, the following three questions are addressed:

Has a mechanism been developed to deal with past atrocities and promote reconciliation between groups?

In past decades, especially in Latin America, many claimed that a public airing of past atrocities and injustices would simply inflame (rather than calm) passions, arguing instead that the best way to rebuild a society after a conflict was to leave the past behind through a mass amnesty that forgave all parties for their actions during the conflict. Today, there is a growing consensus that, at least for the most heinous violations of human rights and international humanitarian law, a sweeping amnesty is not an acceptable solution (Kritz 1996; Orentlicher 1991). However, there is no consensus on whether the perpetrators of such acts should be tried in an international war crimes tribunal, a national court, or allowed to plead forgiveness through a "truth and reconciliation" process.

Whatever the mechanism, the idea is that specific individuals—not entire ethnic groups—committed the atrocities and will be held accountable for their actions. In doing so, it seeks to reject the notion of collective guilt and retribution that all too often produces further cycles of resentment and violence (Kritz 1996). Additionally, the process of bringing out evidence in a trial or airing it in a public forum often provides victims with a sense of justice and catharsis, allowing them to put their rage to rest rather than letting it smolder, ready to break out if given the opportunity (Hirsch 2001).

Have efforts been made to (re)establish local governance, encourage the development of civil society, and promote community-building activities in general?

While certain national institutional designs (such as federal arrangements) may alleviate the worst fears of minority groups, issues such as local control over the use of languages, access to jobs, and the curriculum in local schools give minorities a sense of control over their destiny. Additionally, local governments often are able to form and begin activities even before many national matters are resolved. Basic issues such as policing, economic development, and education can be organized and implemented locally, provided a source of funding can be found.

Do citizens support belonging to the political entity?

Again, while certain institutional designs can increase the role that disaffected groups might play in future governance, they may be of limited use if a portion of the population (especially a majority) does not want to remain a part of the political unit. If the wish is to democratize the country, Robert Dahl (1989, 207) highlights an important problem: "We cannot solve the problems of the proper scope and domain of democratic units from within democratic theory. Like the majority principle, the democratic process presupposes a unit. *The criteria of the democratic process presupposes the rightfulness of the unit itself.* If the unit itself is not [considered] proper or rightful—if its scope or domain is not justifiable—then it cannot be made right simply by democratic procedures." [Emphasis in original.] Although the international community may impede formal recognition of a new entity, a stable state will not be able to develop if there is no commitment on the part of large segments of society to the political unit.

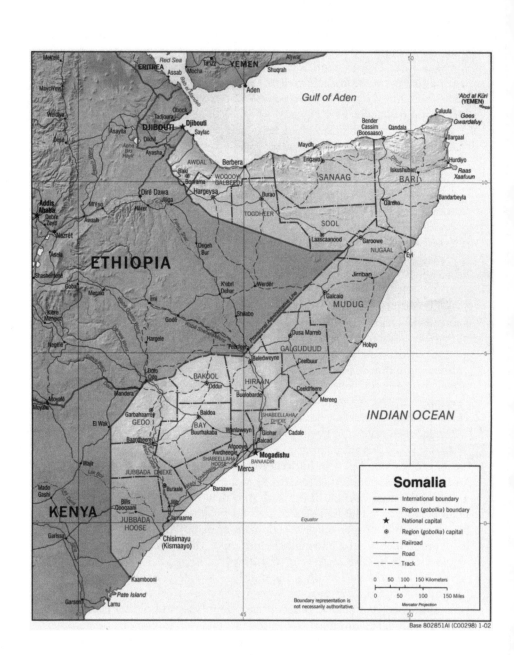

Base 802851AI (C00298) 1-02

CHAPTER 3
SOMALIA

After a largely successful international effort to expel Iraqi military forces from Kuwait in 1991, the international community had high hopes that its newly found collective voice would be successful in resolving many of the other conflicts around the world. Events in Somalia quickly dashed those hopes.

Faced with a civil war and the impending starvation of hundreds of thousands of people, external actors organized a relief operation only to find it thwarted by local warlords. Buoyed by a U.S.-led military effort that brought about a cessation of the violence and allowed the aid to reach the needy, the UN mission that followed was given a broad mandate to rehabilitate Somali governance. However, the mission was given few resources, had little political will to back it up, and found itself increasingly challenged by militia factions. After a number of peacekeepers were killed and a high-profile effort to capture the strongest militia leader was unsuccessful, the larger powers pulled out of the UN military mission, effectively dooming any attempt to rebuild the Somali state.

BACKGROUND OF THE CONFLICT

In the period before colonial rule, ethnic Somalis largely were a pastoral and nomadic society spread across the Horn of Africa, moving about in search of water and forage for livestock as frequent droughts plagued the region. Limited farming was undertaken in the area between the Jub and Shebelle Rivers in the south, while a small trading class lived along the Red Sea coast. With the exception of small Bantu communities, the region was ethnically and religiously homogeneous.

Somalia clans have been compared to Greek and Hebrew tribes, sharing a common ethnic and linguistic identity, but distinguished from one another by lineage, history, and custom (Hirsch and Oakley 1995). Somali society is composed of five principal clan families: the Hawiye, Darod, Isaaq, Dir, and Rahanwein. Each clan is divided into five or more smaller clans, which, in turn, divide into subclans.

Although the coastal peoples were in frequent contact with Arab traders, the Horn of Africa largely was isolated from European colonizers until the mid-1800s. However, the opening of the Suez Canal in 1869 brought the region into European colonial competition. Under the Conference of Berlin in 1884–1885, Italy, Great Britain, and France each staked a claim to a portion of the Horn of Africa inhabited by Somalis. After World War II and the ensuing decolonization, ethnic Somalis ended up in five territories that eventually became a part of four states. Those in the territory controlled by the French ended up in the state of Djibouti. Those in the southern and eastern regions of the Horn controlled by Great Britain ended up in Kenya and Ethiopia (Britain had given Ethiopia the Ogaden region in 1897). Somalis in the coastal area of the Gulf of Aden under British control (what was known as British Somaliland) were joined with the former Italian colonial area along the Indian Ocean to form the state of Somalia, which became independent in 1960. The five-pointed star on the Somali flag represents these Somali territories, although only two are included in present-day Somalia.

The country of Somalia got off to a rocky start, as its northern and southern regions had inherited different European languages, cultures, and administrative structures, and there were no accepted political norms or trained civil servants to administer the country (Hirsch and Oakley 1995). As parties jockeyed for power and development progressed slowly, Somali leaders became frustrated with the perceived lack of support from Western nations and began to seek support from the Eastern Bloc. Part of the reason for the Western reluctance to support Somali leaders, especially in their requests for military hardware, was due to the country's irredentist claims that the areas in which Somalis formed ethnic majorities in Djibouti, Kenya, and Ethiopia should be incorporated into Somalia.

In 1969, as support from the Soviet Bloc increased, a bodyguard assassinated Somali President Abdi Rashid Ale Shermarke, and the feeble democracy fell to a military coup led by Major General Mohamed Siad Barre. From the outset, Siad Barre sought to procure the military equipment that would be necessary to reclaim the Somali areas outside of Somalia. Although Siad Barre initially enjoyed broad public support as he undertook a massive literacy campaign and instituted a written form of the Somali language (rejecting colonial languages), his regime became increasingly authoritarian and relied heavily on trusted supporters from his Marehan clan.

In October 1977, Siad Barre launched an incursion into the Ogaden Region of Ethiopia. However, the Western-oriented feudal regime of Emperor Haile Selassie had been overthrown three years earlier by the only functioning institution in that country: the military. Led by Mengistu Haile Meriam, the Ethiopian military had adopted a Marxist model of development, and the Soviets quickly assisted Mengistu in defeating the Somali army. In response, Siad Barre expelled the Soviet advisors from Somalia and, as his country's economy suffered greatly due to mismanagement and the failure of collectivized agriculture, turned back to the West for aid.

Coming at the same time as the Iranian revolution, Somalia's overtures were well received by the United States, which needed a new base of operations in the Middle East and saw the strategic value of Somalia in the context of the cold war. Not only did a friendly Somalia help protect the sea-lane of communication (SLOC) to and from the Suez Canal, it also provided the United States with a strategically located airfield and port facilities in northern Somalia (that had been used by the Soviets) and a way to keep Soviets in Ethiopia from attempting to broaden their reach.

By 1985, Somalia was the second largest recipient of U.S. assistance in sub-Saharan Africa. Although much of this money went to military assistance, part was directed at a large-scale infrastructure development program to improve the domestic economy. However, internal Somali problems continued to undermine the economy and foster dissension among the Somali people. In trying to keep the opposition weak and divided, Siad Barre manipulated clan politics, playing one clan off against another as his army and police increasingly relied on repression to maintain power.

Somalia essentially slid into civil war in 1988, as northern opposition movements coalesced into the Somali National Movement (SNM) and took over the two largest northern cities, Burao (Burco) and Hargeisa (Hargeysa). The northerners, most of whom were from the Isaaq clan, resented the southern leadership of the country, believing their resources were being funneled away from them to the south, and saw no means of redressing the system through existing institutions (Sahnoun 1994). Siad Barre's government responded by using aircraft and heavy weapons to destroy a large portion of the two cities and much of the infrastructure in the northern regions of the country. An estimated 300,000 Isaaqs sought refuge in Ethiopia and many others were internally displaced (Hirsch and Oakley 1995). In May 1990, 144 well-known and moderate leaders across the country signed a manifesto blaming the government for atrocities and calling for a multiparty system, constitutional changes, and a national conference that would form a caretaker government and prepare for elections. Siad Barre met this direct challenge to his rule by arresting and imprisoning many of the manifesto's signatories, including the former president of Somalia, Adam Abdullah

Osman. Although the United States suspended military assistance to the country and there were some limited moves by the Italians and Egyptians to mediate the problems in Somalia, there was no concerted action by the international community to head off the growing discord in the country (Sahnoun 1994).

By the end of 1990, civil war consumed the entire country as many southern clans also became disaffected with Siad Barre's rule. On January 5, 1991, the United States dispatched helicopters from Desert Storm deployments in order to evacuate U.S. embassy personnel, foreign diplomats, and other aid personnel from Mogadishu. Three weeks later, Siad Barre was forced to flee Mogadishu as United Somali Congress (USC) forces, led by General Mohamed Farah Aideed, entered the city. Siad Barre and his forces moved southwestward to his clan's homeland near the Somali border with Ethiopia and Kenya, but continued attempts to retake Mogadishu. Each time, Aideed's forces repelled him. Frustrated, Siad Barre's fighters pursued a scorched-earth policy, plundering agricultural food stores, gutting tube wells, destroying canals, and rendering agriculture impossible (Hirsch and Oakley 1995; Drysdale 1997). Ravaged by the conflict, farmers abandoned their fields, precipitating a famine. Many of the displaced people fled into what became known as the "triangle of death"—between Mogadishu, Baidoa (Baydhabo), and Bardera (Baardheere)—and became essentially hostages to militia leaders who prevented them from leaving the area and used starvation as a weapon of manipulation. Although Siad Barre eventually fled into Kenya (and on to Nigeria, where he later died), those who had opposed him jockeyed for power, resulting in the increased destruction of the countryside.

Ali Mahdi, one of the signatories of the manifesto, was appointed provisional president by a group of civic leaders, but other groups rejected his appointment. His chief rival was Aideed, whose claims to national leadership largely were based on his military strength and his defeat of Siad Barre's army. Both Ali Mahdi and Aideed were members of the United Somali Congress and the Hawiye clan, although they belonged to the two different subclans that dominated Mogadishu. What was widely judged from the outside as a clash of personalities and ambitions also involved an attempt by Aideed and his subclan members to extend their influence over the rich land in the Shabelle and Jubba Valleys (Clarke 1997).

In the context of this national chaos, the northern region (what had been the former British Somaliland) announced it was seceding from Somalia. Believing that the north would continue to be victimized by any southern-dominated government, the region declared its independence as the Somaliland Republic in May 1991. While not recognized internationally, the de facto secession split the country in two and allowed the northern area to establish a relative sense of stability (Hirsch and Oakley 1995).

In July 1991, an attempt to promote national reconciliation was undertaken by Djibouti. At the conference, Ali Mahdi was confirmed as president for two years. Aideed, who had boycotted the conference, immediately rejected its outcome. Though it had been intended to alleviate the standoff, this triggered open warfare in Mogadishu. Much of Ali Mahdi's support came from urban dwellers in Mogadishu where he had been a businessman, while large portions of Aideed's support came from nomads who had fought with him in the Ogaden when he had been a general in Siad Barre's army. Hirsch and Oakley (1995) point out that this difference created a strong reaction among Aideed's supporters against what they saw as the luxury and self-serving attitudes of Ali Mahdi's followers and led to great property destruction and indiscriminate violence.

EFFORTS BY EXTERNAL ACTORS

Throughout 1991, Somalia competed with other high-profile events for international attention. The impending demise of the Soviet Union and wars in the Persian Gulf and the Balkans left little time for consideration of the plight of the Somalis in international decision-making circles. Although Somalia was not totally ignored, there were no serious discussions at the United Nations or in the United States during that year of doing more than delivering humanitarian aid to the country. The Organization of African Unity (OAU) had rebuffed UN involvement in Sudan and Liberia and did not favor a political role for the United Nations in Somalia. The argument that more extensive UN action was an intrusion into the country's sovereignty repeatedly plagued international efforts to deal with the crisis. Many countries were reluctant to support an international intervention into a country's internal problems without that state's consent, fearing it would set an untenable precedent.

Outgoing UN Secretary-General Javier Perez de Cuellar dispatched Under-Secretary-General James Jonah on a fact-finding mission, while Egyptian Boutros Boutros-Ghali prepared to take over as secretary-general in the beginning of 1992. Boutros-Ghali strongly believed that the United Nations should be the "central instrument for the prevention and resolution of peace" (Boutros-Ghali 1992a). When the United Nations adopted its first resolution (Resolution 733[1]) on Somalia in January 1992, there was no semblance of national structure in the country. The resolution called for a total arms embargo and urged the conflicting parties to agree to a cease-fire and promote a process of reconciliation. It also called on the international community to increase humanitarian assistance to the country and on the feuding parties to facilitate the distribution of that aid and ensure the safety of those delivering it. However, as the civilian death toll steadily mounted, it became apparent that the ad hoc distribution of relief supplies in the anarchic environment was not working.

The United Nations bolstered its efforts in March 1992, when veteran Algerian diplomat Mohamed Sahnoun was dispatched to Somalia as the special representative of the UN secretary-general (SRSG). The following month, the UN Security Council established the United Nations Operation in Somalia (UNOSOM). Resolution 751 called for the immediate deployment of fifty UN observers to monitor the cease-fire that had been signed two months prior, agreed in principle to establish a UN security force to be deployed as soon as possible, and called on the secretary-general to facilitate the effective cessation of hostilities throughout the country to promote the process of reconciliation and political settlement. It also created a committee to report on the implementation of the arms embargo imposed in January and called on the international community to support a ninety-day Plan of Action for Emergency Humanitarian Assistance to Somalia.

This was the first time the United Nations had authorized (in accordance with Chapter VI of the UN Charter, which dealt with the peaceful resolution of disputes) a peacekeeping mission to an area in which there was no legitimate government to provide consent. Under this authority, peacekeepers were to be lightly armed and only use force in self-defense.

In July, after Secretary-General Boutros-Ghali (1992b) berated members of the Security Council for "fighting a rich man's war in Yugoslavia while not lifting a finger to save Somalia from disintegration," the Security Council endorsed a proposal for an emergency airlift of food and medical supplies into the "triangle of death" in the southern part of the country. The United States responded by undertaking Operation Provide Relief, which airlifted humanitarian relief supplies into the region and authorized the transport of the first five hundred peacekeepers to Somalia.

These efforts increased the hopes among the people in Somalia that the international community was finally coming to their aid. However, the assistance was limited and slow in coming. Although the airlift was able to move supplies into the interior, the local militias quickly adopted a practice of extorting landing fees and looting the supplies. Shifting to a strategy of arranging "airdrops" of supplies to the nongovernmental organizations (NGOs) in different areas, the airlift contributed to a lessening of the crisis, but was not able to meet the massive needs of the population. The food and supplies that did arrive through the port facilities were often held in warehouses at the port with no secure way to move them into the needed areas. That which was shipped out often was stolen along the way and resold at high profits.

As the situation deteriorated over the summer, the secretary-general dispatched another fact-finding mission to the country. His report from that mission stated that UN efforts to date were "in no way adequate to meet the overall needs of the Somali people. Present estimates, which may be conservative, indicate that as many as 4.5 million people are in desperate need of food and other assistance" (Boutros-Ghali 1992c). In August, Sahnoun finally was able to secure formal agreement from Aideed to allow the five hundred Pakistani peacekeepers to enter Mogadishu. However, two weeks later, the UN Security Council—with no advance warning to Sahnoun or Aideed—approved the secretary-general's request to expand the number of peacekeepers to three thousand. Aideed thought he had been deceived. When the five hundred Pakistanis arrived in September, they were largely restricted to the airport, hobbled by stringent rules of engagement, and unable to carry out their mission (Hirsch and Oakley 1995). Aideed was convinced that the increased number of peacekeepers was motivated by more than humanitarian concerns, and that its real intention was to undermine his base of power and impose a UN trusteeship over the country (Drysdale 1997).

In October, a one-hundred-day plan was initiated for accelerated relief deliveries to Somalia involving UN agencies, donor countries, the Red Cross, and various NGOs. The UNOSOM team led by Sahnoun actively negotiated with clan leaders, elders, and various groups in Somalia society to gradually reduce the fighting and allow food deliveries into the interior. Sahnoun repeatedly expressed his frustration with the slow response of the UN headquarters to his urgent pleas for more aid, and claimed that the inability of the UN agencies to meet their pledges undermined his credibility among the Somali people.

At a donors' conference convened in Geneva, Switzerland, in October 1992, Sahnoun (recounted in his 1994 memoirs) pointed out that the delivery of relief assistance and the security arrangements that they were able to negotiate were stopgap measures. Without national reconciliation, he claimed Somalia would become a "bottomless pit" into which the donor community would continue to pour humanitarian assistance with no end in sight. He also stated that many respected elders had repeatedly requested assistance in the disarmament of the population and the demobilization of irregular forces, claiming there were too many elements with a vested interest in disorder. Over the summer and early fall, Sahnoun's relations with UN headquarters in New York began to fray. While his style of establishing personal contacts with all factions won him the appreciation of many Somalis, Sahnoun increasingly became viewed at UN headquarters as too independent a player (Hirsch and Oakley 1995). His requests for greater flexibility, increased resources, travel outside of Somalia, and his public criticism of UN headquarters rankled senior members of the Secretariat and UN agencies. Sahnoun, on his part, found himself having to report to three under-secretaries—for peacekeeping, political affairs, and humanitarian affairs—with only minimal coordination and direction from the secretary-general. Additionally, since the UN agencies in the field were not operationally responsible to Sahnoun, they were inclined to resist his authority (Hirsch and Oakley 1995).

In late October after receiving cables from the secretary-general questioning his travels and ordering him to refrain from further criticism of the UN headquarters and its various agencies, Sahnoun submitted his resignation, effective immediately. In his letter of resignation he offered to remain in Somalia to serve as a special envoy to address specific problems, but received no response from the secretary-general. Sahnoun's rapid departure compounded UNOSOM's logistical and personnel problems, probably increased Somali distrust of the United Nations, and undoubtedly represented a major setback to prospects for a political resolution of the crisis (Stevenson 1993).

Between 1988 and November 1992, estimates are that more than a half-million Somalis perished due to fighting, famine, and disease.[2] The U.S. State Department's Office of Foreign Disaster Assistance (OFDA) reported that 25 percent of southern Somali children under the age of five had already died. In the southern city of Biadoa (in the "triangle of death"), the U.S. Center for Disease Control reported that 40 percent of the entire population and 70 percent of its children under the age of five had perished. As the media increasingly reported on the dire conditions, members of the U.S. Congress, NGOs, and the public put increasing pressure on then U.S. President George Bush to "do something" to deal with the situation. Reluctance of the United States to become more actively involved resulted from a number of factors, including ongoing military activities in the Persian Gulf and Balkans, Somalia's decreased significance due to the end of the cold war, and negative assessments of prospects for a resolution of the crisis by the United Nations.

About six weeks after the United States began conducting the airlift, the Pentagon concluded that the ad hoc approach to Somalia was becoming counterproductive and that long-term planning and better coordination of international efforts were needed. A month later, Chairman of the Joint Chiefs of Staff Colin Powell took the lead in the Defense Department's decision to propose a large-scale U.S.-led military intervention, a complete turnaround from its position earlier in the year (Hirsch and Oakley 1995). This option, along with others to increase U.S. support for UN peacekeeping efforts, and the insertion of coalition of forces without U.S. troop participation, were forwarded to the president without recommendation. Because Bush had recently been defeated in the presidential election, he consulted with President-elect Bill Clinton before he selected Powell's plan. He then dispatched officials to the United Nations to see how the operation could be coordinated with their efforts.

Although some UN officials were initially reluctant to accept the plan, fearing there was too great an emphasis on the use of force, the UN Security Council unanimously adopted Resolution 794 on December 3, 1992, endorsing the "offer of a member state" to lead a multinational force into Somalia for the purpose of "establishing as soon as possible a secure environment for humanitarian relief operations in Somalia." This did not create a UN military force, but authorized a member-led force that came to be called UNITAF (Unified Task Force), pursuant to Chapter VII of the UN

Charter (which deals with the forceful resolution of disputes), to use "all necessary means" to establish a secure environment. Although the resolution called for the establishment of appropriate mechanisms for coordination between the United Nations and the U.S. military forces, it did not address the relationship of UNITAF to UNOSOM or how it would fit into the long-range resolution of the problems in the country.

The following day, President Bush announced the operation at a press conference, followed by briefings from Secretary of Defense Richard Cheney and Powell. The mission objectives, according to Cheney, were the establishment by U.S. forces of a secure environment for the delivery of relief supplies and the consolidation of a security framework so that it could be handed over to regular UN forces after a few months. Clarke (1997) points out that this humanitarian enterprise was developed as a purely military operation with no intention of trying to remedy the political chaos in the country. In fact, he notes that critical civil affairs and military police training components were removed from the package by the U.S. Central Command (CENTCOM), probably because the initial plan was based on the idea that the entire mission would be over within a few weeks ("out by Inauguration Day").

Lieutenant General Robert Johnston (USMC) was designated as the commander of the Joint Task Force with overall control of the mission. To supplement the military's efforts, President Bush appointed Robert Oakley as special envoy to Somalia. Oakley had previously served as U.S. ambassador to the country from 1982 to 1984 and was well known to the political and military officials with whom he would need to work. He was to coordinate all U.S. civilian activities in Somalia; provide political advice to UNITAF; act as a liaison to the newly designated UN SRSG, Ismat Kittani (Sahnoun's replacement); and work closely with the NGO community. Oakley met with Aideed and Ali Mahdi in advance of the marine landing to enlist their cooperation in ensuring that the U.S. forces would not be challenged upon their arrival.

Operation Restore Hope had four phases: the landing of the task force, setting up relief sectors to distribute aid, extending operations southward, and turning over the operation to the United Nations. Phase I involved the marine landing in Mogadishu and establishing control of the port, harbor facilities, and airfields. The amphibious landing went quite smoothly, although the arriving marines found the beaches they had intended to enter upon under the cover of night well illuminated by floodlights from numerous international television crews. Within days, the port and airport were brought under control, repaired, and became operational. Shortly after the amphibious landing, Oakley, Johnston, and Kittani invited the two Somali leaders for a working lunch to clarify what the parties could expect from each other. During the meeting, the Somali leaders (after requesting to meet without the foreigners present) hashed out a seven-point agreement, which they signed and read to the media. However, as the U.S. and UN leaders soon found out, signing an agreement did not mean that either party necessarily intended to keep it (Hirsch and Oakley 1995).

The cease-fire, already theoretically in effect, took hold quickly, although both sides were slow in implementing the provisions to canton heavy weapons (including the so-called "technicals," which were pickups and assorted utility vehicles equipped with various weaponry). Ali Mahdi turned over his weapons in mid-February, signaling his intention to focus on the political aspects of the conflict, while Aideed moved most of his weapons out of Mogadishu to avoid confiscation (Hirsch and Oakley 1995). Given the limited U.S. mandate, which had deliberately excluded the general disarmament sought by the UN secretary-general, the United States did not push the issue so long as the weapons posed no threat to the UNITAF forces or humanitarian operations. U.S. forces operated under reasonably liberal "rules of engagement" (ROE), which defined when and how much military strength could be used in a situation. In addition to self-defense, UNITAF forces were allowed to powerfully enforce four noes: no "technicals," no banditry, no roadblocks, and no visible weapons (Daniel and Hayes 1999).

Phase II entailed dividing southern Somalia into eight humanitarian relief sectors (eventually, a ninth was added) where help was most needed, and was originally planned to be under way fifty days after the initiation of Operation Restore Hope. Although numerous humanitarian relief organizations called for immediate deployments to protect their field operations from the increased intimidation and looting (as groups were eager to seize what they could before the coalition forces arrived), UNITAF resisted, arguing it needed higher force levels before it could undertake the protection of those workers and supplies outside of Mogadishu. However, deployments were completed by the end of December 1992 (less than twenty-five days into the operation) because of the near absence of organized resistance, advance political preparation and intelligence in each of the sectors, and the formidable military reputation established by UNITAF (Hirsch and Oakley 1995).

Phase III extended UNITAF operations south to Kismayo (Kismaayo). By concentrating its efforts in southern Somalia (especially around Mogadishu), UNITAF made Aideed and Ali Mahdi the prominent players in Somalia, minimizing the other factional leaders who controlled large tracts of territory in the country, as well as the traditional clan elders and other non-militarized sectors of Somali society.

Except for minor skirmishes, Mogadishu and a large portion of southern Somalia were relatively stable by the end of January 1993. Although some factional fighting continued to occur around Kismayo and portions of the relief sectors were not fully controlled, UNITAF had largely met its objectives of creating a secure environment for the delivery of relief supplies and consolidating the security framework. However, concerns were growing that the anarchy that had prevailed prior to the arrival of UNITAF would return after its departure, as many weapons caches were hidden, and the factions were neither demobilized nor disarmed. On several occasions, the United Nations had asked the United States to broaden its mission to include the disarming and demobilizing of militias. The United States consistently refused.

As UNITAF attempted to move into Phase IV for the handoff from U.S. forces to UNOSOM II (the subsequent UN peacekeeping operation), foot-dragging on the part of the United Nations was readily apparent. While many had hoped that much of the UNITAF force would be transferred to UNOSOM II under respected Turkish Lieutenant General Cevik Bir, the United States and many other countries that participated in UNITAF had announced their plans to withdraw. The United States appointed Major General Thomas Montgomery as deputy to Bir and left a thirteen hundred-member Quick Reaction Force (QRF) to provide protection for UNOSOM II forces, but placed them under USCENTCOM (U.S. Central Command) in Florida, not under General Bir.

Serious plans for the transition between UNITAF and the UN forces began in mid-March 1993. Oakley had left his post on March 3, intending to send a message to the Somalis that the United Nations had the long-term responsibility to resolve their problems. On March 26, the UN Security Council adopted Resolution 814—the first drafts of which had been written in the Pentagon—that formally created UNOSOM II (Clarke 1997). This was the first time in history that a peacekeeping force was established under Chapter VII provisions of the UN Charter. The resolution called on the force to provide for the "consolidation, expansion, and maintenance of a secure environment throughout Somalia" and for "the rehabilitation of the political institutions and economy of Somalia." U.S. Ambassador to the United Nations Madeleine Albright claimed that this was an "unprecedented enterprise aimed at nothing less than the restoration of an entire country" (United Nations 1993).

Despite numerous pleas by the UN secretary-general and his newly designated special representative to Somalia, Jonathan Howe (an American who replaced Kittani), U.S. forces by and large completed their departure by May 4, 1993. Despite the broad mandate of the UN resolution, little specific guidance was given to Bir and Howe on rules of engagement, command and control issues, or coordination of the political and military functions. Although many of the promised troops had not arrived, the new UN commander had more forces in Mogadishu than had Johnston the previous month. However, essential planning on logistics, engineering, and intelligence had not been done, and coordination among the military, political, and humanitarian groups broke down as the United Nations created a bureaucratized organization with clearly separated functions (Hirsch and Oakley 1995).

Although many of the U.S. operations had been conducted out of areas near the port and airport in Mogadishu—areas under Aideed's control, which led to rumors that UNITAF had a special relationship with him—Aideed believed that foreign actions had favored Ali Mahdi from the outset (Drysdale 1997). The new UN leaders compounded that distrust when UNOSOM II refused to support a peace conference Aideed had called in mid-May and instead arranged for rival faction leaders to attend a parallel UN-arranged one. UNOSOM had concluded that Aideed's ambitions could never be satisfied by power sharing and compromise, and decided that he should be marginalized rather than engaged in high-level dialogue (Clarke 1993).

Feeling confident that the Pakistanis who had replaced the U.S. Marines in southern Mogadishu were less capable, Aideed responded by making his Somali National Alliance (SNA) militia more prominent on the streets and using his radio station to condemn the United Nations as interfering in internal Somali politics. UNOSOM decided to close Aideed's radio station and informed him that a UN team would inspect his weapons depots the next day. Accordingly, on June 5, 1993, Pakistani forces entered the radio station, which was located at one of the weapons storage locations. Fighting broke out, but the UN force was able to complete its inspection and withdraw. However, hostile crowds began forming at that site and elsewhere in southern Mogadishu. Pakistani soldiers were ambushed on a road, while angry mobs confronted Pakistani patrols. Elements of U.S. and Italian forces were called upon to assist the Pakistanis, who were pinned down. When the fighting ended, some twenty Pakistanis were dead and many more wounded. The crowds mutilated many of the bodies.

The UN Security Council convened an emergency session the following day and stated that it was "gravely alarmed at the premeditated murder of UN peacekeepers launched by forces apparently belonging to the United Somali Congress (USC/SNA)." Resolution 837 authorized all necessary measures to be taken against those responsible for inciting such attacks, including their arrest and detention for prosecution, trial, and punishment. Aideed's faction had now become the enemy of the United Nations.

The deaths of the peacekeepers greatly complicated UNOSOM's command and control arrangements. Complaining that there was a lack of adequate consultation, planning, and advance notification by UNOSOM, French forces began following orders from Paris. After the deaths of four Italian peacekeepers in early July, Italy put its forces under its national control as well, and refused to participate in actions against the SNA.

Over the next four months, confrontations between Aideed and the United Nations escalated with increasing casualties among peacekeepers and Somali citizens. After the Moroccan battalion commander was killed, Howe issued a warrant for Aideed's arrest and offered a twenty-five thousand dollar reward for his capture. This infuriated Aideed, effectively ending any hopes for reviving a dialogue between the United Nations and the SNA (Hirsch and Oakley 1995).

On July 12, the U.S. Quick Reaction Force launched a raid using helicopter gunships on Aideed's headquarters, killing numerous Somalis. Although the operation had been planned and recommended by UNOSOM, the U.S. chain of command and UN headquarters had approved it. The raid, however, led many Somalis to view the United States as the enemy (Hirsch and Oakley 1995). On August 8, a remotely controlled device exploded under a U.S. Humvee, killing four soldiers. After six more U.S. soldiers were wounded in an attack the following week, President Clinton ordered Delta Force commandos, Army Rangers, and a helicopter detachment (who would report to CENTCOM) to Mogadishu in order to go after Aideed. Aideed began to take on mythological proportions in the David versus Goliath, cat-and-mouse game.

As violence continued, international and Somali support for UNOSOM decreased and humanitarian operations were significantly reduced as many NGOs evacuated their personnel. Although there was little organized violence, increasing rivalries were seen among the Somali factions as Aideed's Habr Gedr clan and its subclans banded together, fearing attacks by other clans.

In the United States, the Congress and the public became increasingly uneasy about the Somalia operation, especially in light of reports that the famine had been largely alleviated. In late August, Secretary of Defense Les Aspin called for a narrower, more realistic approach to what might be achieved in Somalia and declined to send the tanks and armored personnel carriers that had been requested by General Montgomery. Secretary of State Warren Christopher met with Boutros-Ghali to encourage the United Nations to adopt a more political approach, but the secretary-general reaffirmed his support for the existing policy.

Events on October 3, 1993, brought the issue to a head. After U.S. Rangers captured a number of Aideed's key aides and were evacuating them, SNA militia members shot down two U.S. helicopters. In the subsequent rescue efforts, the Rangers and Delta Force were ambushed and became pinned down in a major firefight. By the time the Quick Reaction Force and UNOSOM helped bring an end to the fighting, eighteen U.S. soldiers had been killed, seventy-eight more wounded, and between five hundred and one thousand Somalis had been killed or wounded. U.S. Army helicopter pilot Michael Durant had been captured, and the body of a U.S. solider dragged through the streets of Mogadishu for all the world's media to see.

Responding to public outrage, President Clinton announced four days later that it had been a mistake for U.S. forces to be drawn into a UN decision to "personalize the conflict," and he reappointed Robert Oakley as special envoy, signaling the administration's intent to refocus on political reconciliation. Along with announcing his modified policy on Somalia, Clinton dispatched additional U.S. troops to protect the ones already

there, encouraged African leaders to work with the Somalis to reach a lasting political solution, and stated that U.S. forces would be withdrawn by
March 31, 1994. Shortly thereafter, Congress voted to terminate funding
for Somali operations on that same date. Showing growing frustration
with Somali operations, many European countries followed suit, announcing their withdrawals as well. France and Belgium said they would
withdraw in December 1993, Turkey in February 1994, and Germany and
Italy with the United States by March 31, 1994. UNOSOM II as a military
force disintegrated. Aideed and the SNA, undoubtedly overjoyed by the
turn of events, called for a unilateral cease-fire and agreed not to molest
the departing forces.

After being pressured by the United States, the UN Security Council
adopted Resolution 885 on November 16, 1993, authorizing the "establishment of a Commission of Inquiry . . . to investigate armed attacks on
UNOSOM personnel" and suspending the call for Aideed's arrest. The resolution also made it clear that a political track was to be pursued. In January 1994, the secretary-general announced that UNOSOM II would now
focus on supporting "Somali initiatives in the political, security, and nationbuilding process." Its forces would engage in "voluntary disarmament"
should any Somalis so choose, the protection of "ports, convoys, and
refugees," and would "not use coercive methods but would rely on the cooperation of the Somali parties" (Boutros-Ghali 1994). Thus, although it remained formally under Chapter VII of the UN Charter, UNOSOM II had
become a traditional peacekeeping operation as normally was authorized
under Chapter VI. The United Nations lobbied strongly for countries to fulfill their commitments to the provision of forces for the operation. While
many did, others agreed to do so only after the United States promised to
provide them with armored personnel carriers. The upper echelons of
UNOSOM leadership—Bir, Montgomery, and Howe—were replaced.

As violence escalated, UNOSOM II forces became increasingly sequestered
because of their concern for self-defense, providing less protection to relief
operations, which, in turn, declined as destruction spread further. By July, the
"technicals" were back on the streets of Mogadishu and the SNA again was
raiding UN convoys. As months passed, little progress was made in resolving
the political impasse, and a growing number of incidents demonstrated
UNOSOM's incapacity in the summer and fall of 1994. The United Nations
announced it would terminate the UNOSOM II mission on March 31, 1995.
Various UN agencies remained in Somalia, along with numerous NGOs to
continue humanitarian operations, but with no military backing.

EVALUATION OF EXTERNAL EFFORTS

Because of the manner in which external intervention took place in Somalia, it is necessary to divide those efforts into three categories: the initial

UNOSOM I effort, from March to December 1992; UNITAF, from December 1992 to April 1993; and UNOSOM II, from May 1993 to March 1995.

In examining the question of whether UNOSOM I was effective in the broad sense of diffusing the humanitarian emergency, it obviously fell short. Aid was slow in coming, and much of it was stolen or looted by the armed factions, while millions of people faced starvation throughout the country.

Created under Chapter VI of the UN Charter, the peacekeeping force was lightly armed and intended to observe and monitor the cease-fire agreement, relying on the consent of the parties. In the absence of cooperation, it was unable to impose order and stability in Somali society and relied largely on moral persuasion to attempt to accomplish its mission. However, in such a multifaceted conflict where warlords were not always in control of their militias, there was not much UNOSOM I was able to do to alter the situation. Hence, chaos and starvation remained the order of the day.

With UNOSOM I's ineffectiveness clearly demonstrated, the United Nations accepted Washington's offer to establish a secure environment for humanitarian relief operations in Somalia. The well-managed UNITAF forces quickly established control and intimidated the ragtag Somali militias, who were smart enough to move their weapons out of the way of the U.S.-led forces. During the five months of the UNITAF mission, relative order was established and food was distributed to the areas most in need. Chester Crocker (1995), who had been the assistant secretary of state for African Affairs from 1981 to 1989, claimed that the intervention averted a larger tragedy and that a quarter of a million Somali lives were saved. When judged according to the limited mission set out for it, UNITAF was a remarkable success.

However, the success of UNITAF encouraged setting the broad mandate for UNOSOM II under Chapter VII, calling for the consolidation, expansion, and maintenance of a secure environment throughout Somalia and for the rehabilitation of the country's political institutions and economy. Aideed quickly tested the new UN force. After numerous clashes between Aideed's militias and UNOSOM II, the UN force showed its weakness after identifying Aideed as the problem and then failing to capture him. As the hunt for Aideed became the focus of UNOSOM II, the humanitarian efforts and rehabilitation of the country were given less attention, leading many countries to reassess their participation. After the United States announced it would withdraw its troops in the wake of the deaths of the Rangers, the brittleness of the mission was evident and many European countries announced their withdrawal as well. From that point on, the lack of support among the major powers for the UNOSOM II mission left it little chance of bringing about any real change in Somalia. The broad mandate—accompanied by a lack of means and a lack of consensus on its implementation—doomed UNOSOM II to a dismal failure.

In considering the more extensive question of how well external actors helped the country lay a foundation for a more capable, effective, and legitimate state, the outcome is more ambiguous, but still generally negative.

Has an Agreement Been Signed to End the Conflict?

Even before the formal authorization of UNOSOM in April 1992, the United Nations and other external actors recognized that providing food and other necessary supplies to Somalia was not going to resolve the country's deeper problems. Between 1991 and early 1995, there were seventeen national-level and more than twenty local reconciliation initiatives, many sponsored by UNOSOM. Although there were some notable advances on the local and regional levels—especially in the northwest (Somaliland)—no national agreement was reached. Some argue that the conflict in the early 1990s was not yet "ripe" for resolution—that the combatants were not adequately weary of war[3]—and that Aideed's forces were not hurting enough to cede their dominant position at the bargaining table (Betts 1994). Others point to several flaws in strategy undertaken by the external actors.

The most prevalent critique of external actor's strategy was the focus on attempting to strike deals among factional leaders rather than clan-based community leaders (Africa Watch 1995; Clarke 1997; Lewis 1993). In general, the argument is that the "warlords" had a vested interest in continued instability and anarchy and would only see their power diminished by a return to peace. Hence, although the warlords found it necessary to pay lip service to peace, privately they thwarted it. A related criticism is that the UN attempts in mid-1993 to marginalize militia leaders—Aideed, in particular—violated the appearance of neutrality and undermined reconciliation efforts.

It is further claimed that external efforts were more fundamentally flawed in that they lacked an adequate understanding of the nature of Somali political culture and worked against rather than with indigenous practices of conflict management (Africa Watch 1995; Lewis 1993; Sahnoun 1994). Many critics point to UNOSOM's widely publicized peace conferences that attempted to promote national reconciliation by negotiating with faction leaders over a matter of days in plush hotels outside of the country. They claim this practice was at odds with the broad-based process of ongoing consultation upon which Somalis traditionally have relied. An exception is generally made for Sahnoun's efforts in 1992, which have been widely praised for being in keeping with traditional practices.

The lack of consistent leadership in the external efforts is another criticism often voiced. Sahnoun arrived in March 1992 and departed in October of that year. His replacement, Kittani, was quickly overshadowed by the arrival of Oakley and UNITAF in December 1992. Oakley left in early

March 1993 and, as UNITAF departed two months later, the United Nations replaced its entire management team. Then, in January 1994, the United Nations again replaced its entire leadership. Thus, the process of gaining the necessary trust of the parties and being able to build on past efforts was continually disrupted, as negotiations had to begin anew with each arrival of new mediators.

Ken Menkhaus (1997), a special political advisor to UNOSOM during 1993 and 1994, asserts that reconciliation efforts also foundered on deeper obstacles. First, he claims that, central to nearly every failed peace conference, was the issue of who had the right to represent whom in Somali peace talks. In the context of the collapsed state and with factional disputes even within clans, it was never clear who possessed the legitimacy to represent groups at the negotiating table, and who possessed the authority to enforce an agreement if one was reached. Related to this was the critical issue of the size, power, and territorial control of the clans relative to one another. Menkhaus claims each clan possessed a vastly inflated view of its numbers and domain and, hence, escalated demands for its rightful share of political representation.

Second, Menkhaus points out that in the context of disputed leadership, Somali political figures frequently viewed peace conferences more as vehicles for enhancing their own status within their clans than for advancing the cause of peace. Sahnoun (1994) commented that he was not always certain whether, given the lack of militia discipline and training, the warlords with whom he was negotiating were in control of the forces they led or were prisoners of them. In this context, the militia leaders sought the publicity garnered from participating in the international peace efforts, but needed to continue providing booty to their fighters to keep their loyalty and, thus, had a vested interest in continued instability.

Third, Menkhaus claims that UNOSOM II ran into conflicts trying to both play mediator and peace enforcer. For peace enforcement, the UN had to be *impartial*—that is, it had to enforce certain rules of the game on all parties concerned. However, when the United Nations branded Aideed an outlaw after the June 1993 deaths of the Pakistani peacekeepers, it could no longer play the role of a *neutral* mediator.

Has the Fighting Ended and Does the State Have Control of the Territory?

Although the U.S.-led UNITAF was able to establish control in the sectors in which it deployed, the two UNOSOM missions were unable to do so. In the absence of a political agreement among the factions, only the overwhelming firepower of UNITAF was able to stabilize the country temporarily. The UNOSOM I peacekeeping force, in hindsight, was clearly inadequate to be sent into an area where there was no peace to keep.

However, in large part due to the success of the effort to expel Iraq from Kuwait, there was a great deal of hope that an international effort would be enough to encourage local parties in Somalia to reach an accommodation without the use of force. Also, this was the first international intervention into the newer form of internal conflict, and little precedent and guidance existed upon which to chart the course. With the inability of UNOSOM II to control the violence and its subsequent departure in 1995, clan fighting has continued until the present.

Have the Combatants Been Disarmed and Demobilized?

UNITAF recognized that disarmament and demobilization needed to occur, but they did not consider those tasks to be their mission. The United States likened its role to that of a paramedic whose job it was to offer first aid and apply a tourniquet until the patient could be placed under a physician who would oversee its long-term rehabilitation (Daniel and Hayes 1999). The physician was to be the United Nations; the United States itself had not signed up to bear the expense and long-term commitment that was needed in a nationbuilding mission. The understanding that disarmament and demobilization were necessary led the Pentagon to include those items in their draft of the mandate for UNOSOM II.

UNITAF did implement some level of disarmament, but its program was specific and limited. By negotiating an agreement with faction leaders to canton or move heavy weapons away from humanitarian operating areas, it reduced the likelihood of confrontation while allowing the aid deliveries to occur. However, while some may see this as passing the buck, there was little consensus within the United States for mounting a more comprehensive effort to rehabilitate Somalia. Presidents Bush and Clinton each had hopes that the United Nations would be able to deal with these messy conflicts in areas beyond the traditional interests of the United States; fresh from the experience in the Persian Gulf, they had expectations it could.

A mission that would have involved disarming, demobilizing, and bringing about a political resolution of the conflict would have necessitated a commitment of many more troops for a much longer period and a recognition that casualties would be incurred. Even if either Bush or Clinton had used his political capital to push for a larger mission (which neither one wanted), it is questionable whether the U.S. Congress and public would have supported such an endeavor. Thus, for the United States to have supported a mission that included the tasks of disarmament and demobilization, the bar may have raised too high for the mission to get off the ground. UNITAF may never have come to exist. Attempting to modify the mission once under way would have required Clinton to do battle with a military that was already uncomfortable with the mission and had gotten off to a rough start with his administration (notably on the issue of gays in the military). With

Somalia reasonably well under control in early 1993, the Clinton administration, beset with numerous higher-priority issues, did not make any serious moves to expand the mission.

However, it is clear that the ease with which the well-armed and well-organized UNITAF was able to accomplish its narrow mandate led to overly optimistic expectations about what UNOSOM II would be able to achieve, especially in light of the limited means at its disposal and the poor organizational accountability of its management.

Have the Basic Structures of the Rule of Law Been (Re)established?

With the outbreak of full-scale civil war in Mogadishu and southern Somalia in early 1991, many policemen returned to their clan areas. Although Siad Barre had corrupted many of the judges across the country, many reports confirmed that Somali's police force was still reliable, and that it was well trained, disciplined, and generally nontribal (Ganzglass 1997; Hirsch and Oakley 1995). However, during the initial UN operation, little attention was paid to reinstituting the police and court systems across the country. With limited personnel and funds, most outside attention was directed at trying to mediate the feuds among the major clans, which the police could not prevent.

Original operational plans for UNITAF included the activation of eight to ten U.S. Army Reserve Civil Affairs units, which would have assisted in the restoration of governmental functions, particularly the police and judiciary. However, in keeping with the narrow mission of UNITAF, this proposal was dropped from the final plan.

In December 1992, the U.S. Liaison Office (USLO, which was headed by Oakley) and UNITAF were approached as to whether they would support the establishment of an interim native police force. Although General Johnston initially was reluctant, fearing "mission creep," he and Oakley came to see that an indigenous force would eliminate the need for UNITAF soldiers to serve as police—an undertaking which often created friction with the local populations—and would create jobs and provide income to otherwise unemployed Somalis (Hirsch and Oakley 1995). SRSG Kittani was reluctant, arguing that national structures first had to be established before local police authority could be devolved.

In January 1993, the United Nations sent in a three-man Police Technical Team (PTT) to examine the situation and determine whether a national police force could be established, to explore what could be done to rebuild the judicial system, and to recommend whether a civilian police component of UNOSOM was desirable. The PTT concluded that a national Somali police force should be established at its pre–civil war level of approximately eighteen thousand to twenty thousand men, and that the force should be monitored and assisted by a five hundred-person UNCIVPOL (UN Civilian Police) contingent. The report considered this "a matter of the highest priority for Somalia" in order to "encourage and assist the economic reconstruction [of Somalia] by creating and maintaining a countrywide secure environment" (cited in Ganzglass 1997). In a report to the UN Security Council pursuant to Resolution 794, the secretary-general reiterated the importance of establishing the police force. However, the secretary-general took no subsequent action on the PTT recommendations and no UNCIVPOL team was dispatched to Somalia.

Despite this setback, on the ground in Somalia, planning went forward and a police committee was established in Mogadishu through negotiations between Oakley, Aideed, and Ali Mahdi. Each faction nominated committee members, who had to have served in the Somali National Police Force for at least two years prior to January 6, 1991, have some degree of literacy, and have had no prior tangible offense against the Somali people. Initially, due to the lack of funds, relief organizations contributed food to pay the police in lieu of salaries. By March 1993, there was a three-thousand-man police force in Mogadishu (and an additional two thousand in the rest of the UNITAF zone).

In contrast to the evolving acceptance of the benefits of having an indigenous police force by the United States and United Nations, the Australian troops that arrived as part of UNITAF came with a solid plan to restore policing in their sector as a matter of priority (Ganzglass 1997; Plunkett 1998). Charged with overseeing the Bay Region (Baidoa), the Australians came with a civil affairs plan and immediately set to work establishing a functioning police and judiciary so that they could ease the security burden on their troops and allow a renewal of economic activity that depended on having a secure environment. Clan elders proposed names of individuals to form a Police Committee, the Australians approved the selections, and the committee, in turn, named police officers who were drawn from the old Somali national police and were then approved by authorities in Mogadishu. The Australians arranged for a police training program, secured two used vehicles for transport, and provided equipment such as radios, uniforms, batons, and whistles. In accordance with UNITAF guidelines, up to 25 percent of the force was allowed to be armed. Former judges were selected with the approval of the Police Committee and, after meeting with elders and determining the penal code was acceptable, the Australians implemented it as law. Police were paid under a food-for-work scheme, and the Australians helped rebuild a complex containing a police station, court, and small prison. Although this police force was not capable of protecting residents against major militia attacks, Ganzglass (1997), a special advisor to the U.S. State Department during the UNITAF mission, claimed that, by the time the Australians left, there were approximately 260 police officers, a court system, and a community that had confidence in the system of law and order.

As part of UN Security Council Resolution 814 (March 1993), UNO-SOM II was to assist in "the re-establishment of national and regional institutions and civil administration in the entire country; . . . the re-establishment of police, as appropriate at the local, regional or national level [and] in the restoration and maintenance of peace, stability and law and order." Shortly thereafter, the chief of UNOSOM's Justice Division drew up a detailed policing plan, and $42 million of a requested $45 million was budgeted. The one-year plan called for a ten-thousand-member police force to be established by October 31 and the development of a mobile quick reaction force on a priority basis. The plan also called for renovation of police stations and modest transport. Operational control was to be under UNOSOM, but would be turned over "as soon as the Somali government is ready to take over responsibility and authority from UNO-SOM" (cited in Ganzglass 1997). An equally ambitious reconstitution of the judiciary was planned.

Kofi Annan, then head of the UN Department of Peacekeeping Operations (DPKO), approved the plan in May. However, without informing SRSG Howe, Annan decided to hold off requesting aid, trainers, and equipment until Somalis set up local, district, and regional councils that would have supervisory authority over the police and judiciary. This decision was fatal to the justice program, forcing funding to be secured on a haphazard basis. The DPKO took the position that policing and judicial functions should not be funded out of its budget because they were humanitarian or developmental activities (Ganzglass 1997). In December 1993, the United States (making an exception to congressional prohibitions against providing official aid to foreign police forces) promised $33 million in training and equipment for policing, but the DPKO still had not issued hiring notices for the vast majority of CIVPOL positions, and the program died.

The U.S. Department of Justice initiated an International Criminal Investigation and Training Assistance Program (ICITAP) in March 1994, as it pulled out its remaining military forces. The first phase involved training and equipping the policemen and refurbishing police assets within Mogadishu and outlying areas. The second phase, which was to develop a police capability throughout the country, was premised on the existence of a stable civil structure over the period of the two-year program and was to begin after sufficient calm was obtained in Mogadishu. ICITAP left in June, three months after it arrived.

Have Refugees Been Repatriated and Internally Displaced People Returned to Their Homes?

During the anarchy in Somalia in 1992, few refugees and displaced persons were seeking to return home and many more were becoming uprooted due to fighting and famine. As UNITAF brought relative calm and order to southern Somalia, the United Nations High Commission on Refugees (UNHCR) requested assistance from U.S. troops in resettling refugees. Although not part of its mission, UNITAF provided limited assistance through the provision of security, surveillance, and de-mining as refugees returned from Kenya. Plans were drawn up to provide some assistance in rebuilding roads, houses, and schools, but UNITAF withdrew before they could be implemented. As UNOSOM II took over, it continued to resettle refugees, but the numbers dwindled as fighting renewed.

Have Political Authority and Institutions Been (Re)established in a Manner That Allows the Citizens of the Country to Hold Them Accountable for Their Actions?

Only UNOSOM II had as its mission the "re-establishment of national and regional institutions and civil administration in the entire country" (UNSC Resolution 814 [1993]). However, in the absence of a peace agreement and cease-fire among the domestic combatants and an agreed-upon notion of what form the state should take, external actors could do little to reestablish political authority and institutions, let alone worry about ensuring they were accountable to the citizens.

Additionally, some of UNOSOM's efforts to revive Somali state structures worked at cross-purposes with its reconciliation efforts, ending up fueling conflicts instead of resolving them. For example, while different clans were often able to coexist in relative peace in a single location, if they were asked to form a local governmental structure with a fixed number of seats, they often fell into heated disputes, sometimes ending in casualties, while dramatically worsening local security (Menkhaus 1997).

Is Economic Development Underway?

In Somalia, the clan-based conflict is in part a cover for—and symptom of—competition for a declining resource base (Cassanelli 1997). While the country's richest farmland lies in the Jubba and Shabelle regions in the south, politically and militarily weaker clans largely populate these areas. In this environment, it is not surprising that the more powerful clans began to wrest control from the weaker ones. While this trend can be traced to the early 1970s, the civil war greatly reduced constraints on strong-armed tactics, and increased the incentive to seize by force. Although the United Nations and United States were largely preoccupied by the struggle in Mogadishu (and to a more limited extent in Kismayo), this focus ignored many smaller battles for control of land in the countryside.

Although there were some elements of clan vendetta, Cassanelli (1997) views the takeover as more of a struggle by the new "warlords" to seize land resources. In order to attract soldiers, faction leaders promised good farmland in the riverine areas to recruits who would kill or run off the area's farmers. However, other factions frequently responded, either to regain the lost land or to seize it for themselves. If a clan was not able to push others out, it often sought to co-opt or extract payments from local leaders, claim a percent of the harvest, or skim off international aid. In the process, crops were often destroyed or lost, as no one was able to tend or harvest what remained.

In addition to the anarchy in Somalia after the collapse of Siad Barre, a serious drought began in the southern region in late 1991. Andrew Natsios (1997), the assistant administrator of the U.S. Agency for International Development during the Somali crisis, claims these two factors worked together to produce the massive starvation. If the fighting had not been occurring, relief could have been provided more effectively.

The collapse of the state also affected the economic situation in other ways. For example, cattle exports, the largest source of export revenue in the country, dropped dramatically as there was no systematic inspection of cattle. Importers turned elsewhere or paid very low prices for Somali beef.

Because food was so scarce, its value rose dramatically. International relief supplies became very attractive to plunderers, who resold them on the Somali market for huge profits. The profits, in turn, reinforced the power of warlords by giving them more wealth with which to keep followers loyal, purchase more weapons, and capture the loyalty of other unallied clans. Stealing became a common way of life and the economic system was built around it. With no court system, no police force, and no way of protecting themselves, the NGOs and relief agencies believed they had little choice but to hire large numbers of locals and pay off militia leaders to protect their convoys and distribution centers. However, this tactic further increased the market for weapons and ammunition. Thus, NGOs created a premium for armed men at a time when unemployment was high and weapons were cheap and in ample supply, in large part due to the collapse of the neighboring Ethiopian regime in 1991. Many people made more money in the context of the chaos than they could hope to during peace. In this respect, international aid helped perpetuate the conflict, strengthen the most destructive elements of society, and undermine the stabilizing forces and authority of the traditional clan elders.

In order to counteract these perverse side effects of international assistance, the U.S. State Department (through the Office of Foreign Disaster Assistance [OFDA] and USAID) undertook a number of measures. First, it sought to flood the country with food in order to drive prices down, and to "monetize" a portion of it, meaning food aid would be sold at a reduced price in commercial markets. Also, they sought to replace highly valued commodities such as rice with less-valued ones like sorghum, bulgur (parched cracked wheat), and maize, and to encourage more soup kitchens. However, the OFDA quickly realized that the soup kitchens deterred people from leaving the displaced persons camps and returning to their villages. This both reinforced the local warlords (primarily Aideed because the most severe famine was in the area under his control) and inhibited the restoration of cattle herds and farming which would create the bases for a revival of the Somali economy. The OFDA then sought to decentralize relief to smaller cities and villages, encourage refugees and internally displaced persons (IDPs) to return to their villages, provide seeds and tools to farmers, and create mass employment programs to repair the necessary infrastructure (such as irrigation ditches), get youths off the street, and get the economy moving again.

However, problems soon arose. The OFDA could not find enough merchants to purchase large quantities of food to monetize it effectively and, instead of reducing violence, the drop in food prices increased it as the warlords and thieves stole more to make up for lost income. It soon became apparent that changing the market dynamics had little impact on the overall security situation (Natsios 1997).

Has a Mechanism Been Developed to Deal with Past Atrocities and Promote Reconciliation between Groups?

Having no system of rule of law in place (and no state capable of enforcing one), Somalia has not attempted to deal with atrocities committed since the outbreak of civil war in 1988.

Have Efforts Been Made to Reestablish Local Governance, Encourage the Development of Civil Society, and Promote Community-Building Activities in General?

Much of the attention of the UNOSOM I and early UNOSOM II missions focused on the development of a national government, with the idea that local power and authority would be devolved once that had been achieved. However, by mid-1993, UNOSOM II officials concluded that national reconciliation could only be achieved if a number of regional conflicts were first defused.

One of the more notable regional efforts was the Jubbaland peace accord signed in August 1993, the first attempt by UNOSOM to resolve a regional conflict and the first to embrace clan elders rather than faction leaders as the key players in peacebuilding (Menkhaus 1997). The simple but critical fact that negotiations were held within the region, allowing delegates to meet daily with their constituencies, legitimized the proceedings in the eyes of the community. And because the conference was kept simple and low-budget, there was little financial pressure on UNOSOM to press for a rapid conclusion. This allowed for a number of informal, social meetings such as "peace feasts" and women's groups, which were designed to bring communities directly back into communication again. Although these efforts may have been facilitated by UNOSOM, the communities themselves always initiated them, helping to reestablish old affiliations between clans and placing social pressure on political elements that distrusted the peace process (Menkhaus 1997). However, the Jubbaland Accord was never fully implemented, and violent conflict broke out again between the two clans in February 1994. In hindsight, Menkhaus claims that neither clan's militia intended to abide by the accord, nor were the elders able to force either to adhere to its provisions.

As set out in the 1993 Addis Ababa agreement, the United Nations facilitated the development of district and regional councils across the country, even though Aideed's SNA opposed their creation. All in all, the United Nations was able to create fifty-two (out of a possible ninety-two) district councils and eight (out of a possible eighteen) regional councils. However, the councils were unable to become institutionalized and rose and fell according to struggles among the militias.

In contrast, the breakaway region of Somaliland was able to construct a reasonably representative, functioning regional government, and has continued to assert its independence from the rest of Somalia. This effort was largely conducted through a series of conferences (with limited external support) by clan elders who held more control over their militias than did clan leaders in the south.

Do Citizens Support Belonging to the Political Entity?

With the notable exception of Somaliland, most Somalis do not contest belonging to the state of Somalia. Most even still hold out hopes that ethnic Somalis in the neighboring states will be joined with them in a larger union. However, the fact they do not wish to leave the state has not made it easy to form a national government.

In the northern region of Somaliland, the division has its roots in the colonial period when the British ruled it while the Italians ruled the southern portion of Somalia. While the theory of ethnic unification exists, practical problems have dogged the country ever since. Although they fear they will be unfairly treated under any government dominated by southerners, in the context of the ongoing chaos, they also believe they will be able to progress much faster as an independent country. Without independence, the region only receives limited international assistance and many private investors are wary of the insecure political and legal framework.

SUMMARY AND CONCLUSIONS

As civil war and famine combined to devastate the Somali people in the early 1990s, external actors intervened in an attempt to end the starvation, develop a political solution to the crisis, and rebuild the institutions of governance. After initial UN efforts proved inadequate, the United States launched Operation Restore Hope in December 1992, led by UNITAF. This effort was able to overwhelm the Somali militias and create an environment in which international assistance could be provided to the starving Somalis. After UNITAF had stabilized the southern area of the country in which it was deployed, control was turned over to a strengthened UN mission (UNOSOM II), which was given a mandate not only to ensure that aid was able to be administered, but also to rehabilitate the political institutions and economy of Somalia. Militia factions who saw their political futures hampered by these efforts began challenging the international force. After dozens of peacekeepers were killed in the summer of 1993, the strongest factional leader, Mohammed Farah Aideed, was branded the problem and a warrant was issued for his arrest.

In the process of trying to capture Aideed, violent clashes took place between Aideed's forces and those of UNOSOM. In August, eighteen U.S. Army Rangers were killed, prompting a reevaluation of U.S. support for the UN operation in Somalia and the subsequent announcement that U.S. forces would be withdrawn by the end of March 1994. Most European countries followed suit, and the UN operation became increasingly weakened with no strong support from any member of the UN Security Council. As militia forces became emboldened, violence grew, prompting the evacuation of many international relief workers. In concluding that conflicts within the dominant Hawiye clan—to which both Aideed and Ali Mahdi belonged— impeded UN efforts to achieve political reconciliation, the United Nations terminated its UNOSOM II operation on March 31, 1995.

In sum, international efforts eventually were able to alleviate the worst of the humanitarian emergency and likely saved, at a minimum, a quarter of a million Somali lives. Longer-term efforts were generally unsuccessful due to the inability of the external efforts to bring about a political resolution of the conflict. Numerous missions were undertaken to try to reach some accommodation, but there was little incentive for Aideed (as the head of the strongest faction militarily) to settle for something that did not give him ultimate power. In the absence of an agreed-upon national government and with a return to civil violence, the attempt to reconstruct the state never really got off the ground. While some aspects of state reconstruction were thwarted by anarchy (e.g., demobilization and disarmament, the repatriation of refugees, and economic development), other parts were partly undermined by insufficient international planning and the commitment to see them through (e.g., development of local police forces).

Much of the lack of success in Somalia can be attributed to the Somali factions themselves. However, the external actors failed to develop an integrated overall political and military approach. Part of this may be excused because Somalia was the first operation of this kind and many lessons were learned the hard way. However, especially with the benefit of hindsight, many of the shortcomings of international efforts can be tied to an overly optimistic expectation of what the United Nations would be able to accomplish when given limited support and means. In this sense, operations in Somalia should not be viewed as proving the failure of the concepts of humanitarian intervention or muscular peacekeeping, but demonstrating that an ambitious mission coupled with limited means and support will be doomed to failure.

NOTES

1. All of the UN Security Council Resolutions are available through the United Nations' website at www.un.org.

2. The figures in this paragraph are taken from Hirsch and Oakley (1995), pp. 31–32.

3. For a discussion of the "ripeness" concept, see Zartman 2000.

CHAPTER 4

BOSNIA AND HERZEGOVINA

As Yugoslavia began breaking up in the early 1990s and warfare ensued, the international community found itself torn between fears of being drawn into a seemingly intractable ethnic conflict and the horror that such barbarism could be occurring in late twentieth-century Europe. Beset by their inability to resolve the conflicts among the Somalis, external actors could not reach agreement on what policies should be pursued in the Balkans.

However, as photos reminiscent of the concentration camps during the Holocaust appeared and widespread reports that ethnic cleansing and even genocide were occurring, concerns grew that the conflict could spread through the southeastern region of Europe, and NATO began to take stronger action. Coupled with a Croatian military advance and a willingness of the Yugoslav president to reach an agreement, a political solution that met everyone's minimum needs—yet satisfied no one—was signed in late 1995, allowing the construction of the state of Bosnia[1] to begin.

BACKGROUND OF THE CONFLICT

Slavic peoples first began conducting raids into—and eventually settling in—the Balkan Region in the sixth and seventh centuries. Over the following centuries, the kingdoms of Serbia, Croatia, and Bosnia were formed. Power struggles between the kingdoms soon developed, and Serbia and Croatia split control of Bosnia in the ninth century. During the eleventh and twelfth centuries, Hungary ruled the region. The kingdoms of Bosnia, Serbia, and Croatia regained their independence around 1200. In the late

1300s, the Ottoman Turks began conquering the area and, by the mid-1400s, dominated the entire region.

Although the Serbs viewed the Muslim Turks as alien occupiers, the Bosnians welcomed them as liberators from the dominating Orthodox Serbs and Catholic Croats. In an effort to keep their land, the Bosnians converted to Islam. This was the first of several episodes in which some local populations of the Balkans welcomed foreign powers as a means of helping their group secure an advantage over local rivals. Bosnia remained under Ottoman rule until 1878, when it was ceded to Austria-Hungary. Serbia became fully independent that same year.

While Bosnia was a part of the Austro-Hungarian Empire, Slavs in Serbia and elsewhere in the region were calling for a South Slav state. In 1914, Austrian Archduke Ferdinand was assassinated in the Bosnian capital of Sarajevo by a Serb terrorist—the so-called "spark" that ignited World War I. After the war, the Kingdom of Serbs, Croats, and Slovenes (which included Bosnia) emerged as a new nation, patched together out of defeated empires and native kingdoms. The new nation emerged as a voluntary union of the Slavic groups in the area and was accepted by the international community in part due to U.S. President Woodrow Wilson's emphasis on the principle of self-determination of peoples in Eastern Europe. In recognition of the role Serbia played in World War I and because of the Serbs' numerical plurality, the Serbian royal house of Karadjordjević was given hereditary rule over the new constitutional monarchy.

Ethnic tensions soon arose in the new country. In 1928, a Montenegrin Serb stood up in Parliament and shot the Croatian leader for insulting the Serbs, leading the Croats to withdraw from Parliament. King Alexander disbanded Parliament, established an absolute monarchy, divided the country's regions without regard to racial composition, and changed its name to Yugoslavia (the name means "south Slavs") in an attempt to promote a Yugoslav identity and downplay rival nationalities.

Invaded and partitioned by the Germans and Italians in World War II, Yugoslavia split into ethnic factions fighting occupiers and fighting each other. The three largest factions were the Croat-dominated "Ustashe," allied with Nazi Germany; the "Chetniks," who were tied to the Serb-dominated Yugoslav government in exile and feared the Communists more than the Nazis; and the "Partisans," led by Josep Broz Tito, who were tied to the Communists. During the war, close to two million Yugoslavs were killed, about half by other Yugoslavs. At the end of the war, Tito emerged as the country's leader and abolished the monarchy, setting up in its place the Communist Federal Republic of Yugoslavia. Tito (who had a Croat father and a Slovene mother) divided Yugoslavia into six republics: Slovenia, Croatia, Bosnia-Herzegovina, Serbia, Macedonia, and Montenegro. However, the lines were not drawn to match the ethnic settlement patterns, and many ethnic communities—particularly the Serbs—found themselves outside of their "titular" republic. It often was said that Yugoslavia consisted of six republics, five nationalities, four languages, three religions, two alphabets, and one Tito.

In 1948, after disputes with Russia, Yugoslavia was expelled from mainstream international communist groups. The United States, driven by geopolitical concerns and the growing U.S.-Soviet rivalry, provided assistance to the country, both to show that countries could break free from the Soviet orbit and to stop the flow of weapons to communist groups in Greece who sought to overthrow the Western-oriented government there. Successive U.S. administrations continued to support Tito (who brutally suppressed all internal dissent) in order to deprive the Soviets of an outlet into the Mediterranean.

Yugoslavia's economy began to take a turn for the worse in the late 1970s, leading to high unemployment and protests, some of which began to take on nationalist overtones. In 1980, Tito died, and the glue that had held the country together for the past three decades was gone. As the Yugoslav government struggled to restructure its economy, political stability was elusive. In 1986, Slobodan Milošević became the president of the Republic of Serbia. He quickly found that fanning the flames of Serbian nationalism enhanced his domestic popularity and, in 1989, he revoked Kosovo's autonomous status that had been granted by Tito in 1974. Although the province was 90 percent ethnic Albanian, Milošević purged many of Kosovo's governing bodies of Albanians and replaced them with Serbs as part of his national campaign to create a "Greater Serbia," a move popular with many Serbians.

In late 1989, the cold war ended, depriving Yugoslavia of the special status that brought in high levels of Western aid and a blind eye to human rights abuses in the country. As the economy declined and Milošević attempted to orchestrate Serb-dominance of the entire country, the republics began demanding increased autonomy. The Slovenes, with relatively close ties to Italy and Austria, resisted all attempts to increase the power of the central government and openly criticized Milošević's Kosovo policies, which earned them an economic blockade.

In the spring of 1990, elections were held across most of the Yugoslav republics. Almost everywhere, local nationalists prevailed. In bringing nationalists to power, the elections helped undermine the foundation of democracy (Zimmerman 1999). In the fragmented Yugoslavia, no political leaders were capable of rallying citizens behind democratic ideals and no institutional design was in place that forced leaders to reach beyond their dominant national group. Often, the only viable alternative to the nationalists was the Communists, with whom most people had had enough.

By mid-1990, two basic principles came into conflict (Steiner 1998; Zimmerman 1999). The first was the principle of territorial integrity based on the 1974 constitution granting federal dominance over matters such as international borders, foreign affairs, and national defense. The second was the principle of self-determination by the dominant ethnic groups within the republics who sought to govern themselves, protect their interests, and protect their rights as peoples. Fearful of the precedent a breakup of the country would set for the Soviet Union, the United States and many European countries sought to encourage a unified Yugoslavia, but made it clear that they would not resort to force to ensure it.

Many journalistic accounts on the breakup of Yugoslavia attribute the rise of nationalism in the late 1980s and early 1990s to the presence within Yugoslavia of different ethnic minorities with a history of mutual animosity. However, while these differences and animosities may have established permissive conditions for the outbreak of ethnic conflict in Yugoslavia, they were not the sole or even the main cause. Instead, economic decline and political conflict helped produce growing uncertainty and insecurity among Yugoslav citizens, laying the foundation for opportunistic Serb politicians to exploit the appeal of nationalism in an attempt to rise to power in the country after the collapse of communism (Daalder 1996; Hagan 1999; Zimmerman 1999). The early success of Serb nationalism led to a surge in nationalistic behavior in other parts of the country (especially in Slovenia and Croatia), where leaders used nationalistic appeals to further their own political ends. With borders of the republics not corresponding to ethnic boundaries and ethnic minorities living in pockets throughout the country, it is not surprising the breakup became a violent one.

In December 1990, Slovenia and Croatia declared they would secede from Yugoslavia in six months unless a more acceptable federal arrangement was developed that allowed greater levels of autonomy. In June 1991—in keeping with their threat—Slovenia and Croatia declared independence. The international community initially reacted coolly as the Yugoslav National Army (JNA) attempted to force Slovenia to stay in the federation. With more than 90 percent of the population Slovene, few Serbs, no border with Serbia, and close ties to Western Europe, fighting only lasted ten days with less than one hundred fatalities before Yugoslavia let Slovenia go its own way. However, the Serb-dominated JNA took a much tougher stand against Croatia's attempt to leave the federation, due in part to the substantial Serb minority that lived in the Krajina Region and wanted to remain part of Yugoslavia. Within weeks, the JNA forces captured nearly one-third of Croatian territory, expelled non-Serbs from much of that territory, and commenced large-scale bombardment of key cities. The United Nations brokered a cease-fire that was accepted by all sides in January 1992.

EFFORTS BY EXTERNAL ACTORS

In addition to the precedent the breakup of Yugoslavia might set for the Soviet Union, international involvement in the Yugoslav conflict was driven by the desire to prevent the spread of war, relieve the suffering of the people, and demonstrate that aggression does not pay (Daalder 1996). However, the international community was never able to agree upon a strategy to deal with the violence, and verbal reprimands did not stop the determined militias on the ground.

Germany began to support bids for independence by Slovenia and Croatia soon after hostilities erupted, arguing that the international community could more legitimately assist an independent country than it could a rebellious province. Germany led the European Community (EC) countries to recognize Slovenia and Croatia as independent states in January 1992. The United Nations originally had taken the position that the recognition of Croatia and any other Yugoslav entity should only be envisioned in the framework of an overall settlement, fearing that premature recognition would lead to even greater violence. However, after the EC recognized the two states, most major powers followed, and a peacekeeping force (the United Nations Protection Force—UNPROFOR) was deployed in Croatia in April 1992 to monitor the January cease-fire arrangements between the Croats and the Yugoslav (Serb) forces.

In the early 1990s, Bosnia had no majority ethnic group. Muslims (often referred to simply as Bosnians, Bosniacs, or Bosniaks) comprised about 43 percent of the population, Serbs about 32 percent, and Croats about 17 percent (Woodward 1995). Emerging from the 1990 elections, President Alija Izetbegović, a Muslim, had sought to ensure that Bosnia remained a multiethnic community and continued to be a part of Yugoslavia. Izetbegović and other Balkan observers feared that the collapse of Yugoslavia would tear Bosnia apart in a tug-of-war between Serbia and Croatia. Croatia's secession had dire consequences for neighboring Bosnia. Fearing that the Serbs would dominate them if they remained in Yugoslavia after the exodus of the Slovenes and Croats, 63 percent of Bosnia's population voted for independence in February 1992. While this support was well over that of a simple majority, it was not nearly as high as in Slovenia or Croatia, and many Serbs and Croats had boycotted the referendum (Steiner 1998). Despite these factors, independence was declared and recognized by the EC and the United States the following month.

The independence declaration prompted Bosnian Serbs to undertake a massive effort to secure as much of the territory as possible for themselves. The ensuing expulsions of Muslims and Croats from their homes in a self-described Serb campaign of "ethnic cleansing," coupled with the establishment of concentration camps and the shelling of cities, led the international community to impose a complete economic embargo on Serbia and Montenegro (the only republics left within the former Yugoslavia) (Daalder 1996).

In addition to diplomatic efforts to end the conflict, the international community attempted to mitigate the humanitarian consequences through a two-pronged strategy of delivering aid to those in need and protecting highly vulnerable populations. Pursuant to UN Security Council Resolution 725, the United States led a coalition airlift named Operation Provide Promise to provide critical humanitarian aid to cities in Bosnia. In June, the mission of

UNPROFOR (which had been deployed in Croatia in April 1992) was expanded, and what became known as UNPROFOR II was deployed in Bosnia. Its mission was to open the airport in Sarajevo and ensure the safe movement of aid and relief workers from the airport into the city. In subsequent months, the Security Council, acting under Chapter VII of the UN Charter, extended UNPROFOR II's mandate to provide for protection of aid convoys throughout Bosnia by "all measures necessary."

In October 1992, the United Nations established a no-fly zone over Bosnia, which the North Atlantic Treaty Organization (NATO) began monitoring. The following month, NATO began maritime operations (Operation Sharp Guard) in support of UNPROFOR's peacekeeping operations and to monitor and enforce the UN economic sanctions and arms embargo on the countries of the former Yugoslavia. Meanwhile, the UN Security Council (through Resolution 795 of December 11, 1992) expanded UNPROFOR's mandate to the Former Yugoslav Republic of Macedonia (which had declared its independence in September 1991) to deter the spread of conflict into that area. Five hundred U.S. troops joined the mission in Macedonia, the only U.S. combat troops to participate in peacekeeping deployments in the Balkans before 1995.

Diplomatic efforts to stop the fighting continued unsuccessfully. In January 1993, the Vance-Owen Peace Plan was presented, but met with opposition from both the Muslims and the Serbs. The plan called for the division of Bosnia into ten provinces, each of which would have substantial autonomy. The Muslims objected, claiming the plan did not provide the central government with sufficient authority and that it sanctioned ethnic cleansing. The Serbs argued that it forced them to give up too much land and that "their" provinces were not contiguous. With both major parties reluctant, the Clinton administration decided it could not support the plan because it considered it too pro-Serb (Sharp 1997). In an effort to maintain some momentum after the failure of the diplomatic initiative, the Western powers and Russia agreed to establish an International Criminal Tribunal for the former Yugoslavia (ICTY) in order to hold individuals accountable for their violent actions and to deter further acts of genocide. The Clinton administration then began pushing for a "lift-and-strike" strategy—lifting the arms embargo on the Bosnian government and striking against Serb forces, which the administration had come to view as the aggressors. The United Kingdom and France adamantly opposed the strategy, fearing it would intensify the war and jeopardize their peacekeeping forces deployed in the region.

In February 1993, the United States formed the U.S. Joint Task Force-Provide Promise to consolidate all U.S. activities in support of the UN mission in Bosnia. Between February 1993 and January 1996, coalition forces delivered more that 176,000 short tons of food, medicine, and supplies, making it the longest lasting airlift in history. This amounted to an average of the equivalent of 13.8 C-130 sorties per day, 45 percent of which were flown by the U.S. Air Force (Wentz 1998). Although a no-fly zone had been authorized the previous October, it was not until March 31, 1993, that the UN Security Council passed Resolution 816, sanctioning its enforcement. To support this resolution, NATO initiated Operation Deny Flight both to enforce the no-fly zone and to conduct strike operations in support of UN peacekeeping forces. In the late spring of 1993, the United Nations created six safe areas around the cities of Sarajevo, Tuzla, Zepa, Gorazde, Bihac, and Srebrenica in order to protect civilians from air or heavy weapons attacks.

By May, the alliance the Muslims and Croats had formed to combat the Serbs had collapsed and calls for the international community to take more concerted action were increasing. In the wake of the Vance-Owen Plan's failure, two other attempts were made—the "Union of Three Republics" plan and a European Union "Action Plan"—but neither was accepted. Each would have partitioned Bosnia into three ethnic-based entities, but differed on the borders and specific provisions.

In February 1994, in violation of the no-fly zone, NATO planes shot down four Serb aircraft, the first military engagement ever by NATO forces. NATO also issued an ultimatum that all heavy weapons within a twenty-kilometer radius of Sarajevo be removed or placed under UN control. Under mounting international pressure, the Muslims and Croats renewed their alliance and signed a federation agreement in March. Limited missile strikes were conducted in support of UNPROFOR on several occasions throughout the year. While UNPROFOR operated under the principle of neutrality, these actions brought them into direct conflict with the Serbs, who used their planes and heavy artillery against the Muslim populations that UNPROFOR sought to protect. In response, the Serbs began taking UNPROFOR soldiers as hostages to deter future air strikes.

In an attempt to broker a settlement, the United States, the United Kingdom, France, Germany, and Russia formed the "Contact Group." The peace plan they put forward in July called for 51 percent of the territory to go to the Muslim-Croat federation and the remaining 49 percent to the Bosnian Serbs; the latter rejected the plan. Violence surged again at the end of 1994, and the international community could not reach a consensus on what to do. Air strikes had only a limited effect, and were halted by the taking of UN peacekeepers as hostages. In May 1995, the air strikes recommenced, and again the Serbs responded by taking UN peacekeepers hostage, this time chaining them to potential targets and allowing the media to broadcast the images worldwide.

UNPROFOR was gradually withdrawn from Serb-dominated areas, and the "safe areas" of Gorazde, Srebrenica, and Zepa were quickly overrun in July 1995, leading to the slaughter of thousands of Muslims (de Jounge Oudraat 1999). However, the tide turned in the latter half of 1995. After a Sarajevo market was shelled in late August—and UNPROFOR troops were out of the reach of Serb forces—NATO pounded Serb targets across Bosnia with more than two hundred sorties, declaring that the bombardment would not stop until Sarajevo was secure. At nearly the same time, Croatian government forces (which partially had been trained and equipped by retired U.S. military officers acting as private citizens) overran the Serb forces in the Krajina Region in Croatia and began expelling Serbs from the area, prompting them to flee into Serbia and Serb-held portions of Bosnia (Shearer 1998). As the previously dominant Serbs began to lose territory and thus became amenable to negotiations, the United States brokered a cease-fire for Bosnia and Croatia in early October 1995 and invited the leaders of Bosnia, Croatia, and Serbia to peace talks in Dayton, Ohio. After weeks of intensive negotiations, the leaders initialed the *General Framework Agreement for Peace in Bosnia and Herzegovina* on November 21 in Dayton, and formally signed the accords in Paris on December 14, 1995.

The Dayton Accords, as they became known, created a federal state comprised of two entities: the Federation of Bosnia and Herzegovina, which would administer 51 percent of the country; and the Republika Srpska, which would control the remainder. The country would be headed by a tripartite presidency containing one Muslim, one Croat, and one Serb, each holding veto power over the most important matters. The civilian aspects of the accords were to be monitored by the High Representative, who was appointed by the backers of the Dayton Accords and would control seventeen hundred members of the UN International Police Task Force (IPTF) deployed in Bosnia. In the annex, which detailed military aspects of the peace settlement, the United Nations Security Council was invited to adopt a resolution (forthcoming as UNSC Resolution 1031) that would authorize NATO to enforce the terms of the agreement. The NATO Implementation Force (IFOR) was a heavily armed force of sixty thousand soldiers designed to monitor the cease-fire; maintain a separation of Serb, Bosnian, and Croat forces; collect heavy weapons; provide a secure environment; and ensure freedom of movement.

The peace operation was a first for NATO in many respects. Code-named Operation Joint Endeavor, IFOR was NATO's first ground force operation, its first deployment "out of area," and its first joint operation with NATO's Partnership for Peace members and other non-NATO countries, including Russia (Wentz 1998). To some, however, it was ironic that well-armed and well-trained NATO soldiers were deployed to keep the peace only after the agreement was signed, while lightly armed and less-coordinated UN peacekeeping forces had been sent into the country during the conflict when there was no peace to keep.

EVALUATION OF EXTERNAL EFFORTS

The external intervention was successful in diffusing the humanitarian emergency in the short term, but only after a lengthy period of "muddling through." Although there was growing awareness of the seriousness of the

Bosnian conflict in the early 1990s, little consensus existed in the international community on the best course of action. To be fair, numerous other high-profile events competed for decision makers' attention, including the impending disintegration of the Soviet Union, the Gulf War, European integration, the movement to majority-rule in South Africa, famine and civil war in Somalia, and the U.S. presidential elections. Although the responses may have prevented a worse humanitarian catastrophe, they also likely prevented the international community from taking more concerted action to stand up to aggression and nationalism in order to end the conflict. However, in the late summer and fall of 1995, conditions emerged that prompted a settlement to be reached by the ethnic leaderships. In the aftermath of the Dayton Accords, large-scale violence was ended with the presence of sixty thousand well-armed troops from NATO, and a massive civilian relief effort was undertaken to help the Bosnian people rebuild their lives.

There is no simple answer as to whether external intervention has laid the foundation for a more capable, effective, and legitimate state that could avert a relapse into violence. Portions of the peace agreement have been carried out, but fundamental differences remain between the groups, and many see the international effort as being the only glue holding the country together (Bildt 2001; Bugajski 2000; Daalder and Froman 1999; GAO 2000).

Has an Agreement Been Signed to End the Conflict?

The *General Framework Agreement for Peace in Bosnia and Herzegovina* (GFAP) signed in December 1995 essentially ended the armed conflict between the ethnic groups as NATO troops were deployed to implement its military provisions. The peace treaty was designed not only to end the fighting, but also included a constitution for the country and set out provisions for the conduct of elections, the protection of human rights, and the rights of return for refugees and displaced persons. However, although the document is comprehensive in places, in others it is ambiguous, incomplete, and even contradictory, leaving many of the details to be resolved in the implementation period (Cousens 2001a; ICG 2001a).

Many argue that the Croatian military successes in the Krajina Region coupled with concerted international action in the form of sustained NATO air strikes brought the three groups to the bargaining table in Dayton. However, Carl Bildt (2001), the external actor's first high representative in Bosnia, claims that a concrete and realistic plan to end the conflict by the major actors in the international community—the United States, Europe, and Russia—brought the parties to the table. He adds that the key to the settlement was the U.S. acceptance of a highly autonomous Republika Srpska within the framework of a very loose Bosnian state. In this respect, the deal met the minimum demands of everyone, and gave the maximum demands to none.

Although the parties theoretically agreed to all of the provisions in the accords, the Bosnian Serb leaders did not participate in its negotiations or signing, but instead were represented by the president of Serbia and Montenegro, Slobodan Milošević. Many international observers saw Milošević as the one who supplied, funded, and directed the Bosnian Serb leadership. Additionally, because the war crimes tribunal had indicted the top leadership of the Bosnia Serbs, they were not allowed to participate. While Milošević may have been able to deal with the major issues in conflict, the leadership in Republika Srpska often has refused to implement a number of the treaty's more intrusive provisions, such as the restructuring of local police forces.

The mandate for the NATO-led IFOR expired on December 20, 1996, and the North Atlantic Council (the decision-making authority for NATO) announced it was willing to organize and lead a Stabilization Force (SFOR) for an additional period of eighteen months. SFOR was authorized under Chapter VII by UNSC Resolution 1088, which called for its establishment as the legal successor of IFOR, effective December 20, 1996. Although its mandated strength was around thirty-one thousand soldiers—about half of that of IFOR—SFOR operated under the same rules of engagement and was tasked to deter or prevent a resumption of hostilities or other threats to peace, consolidate IFOR's achievements, promote a climate in which the peace process could move forward, and provide selective support to civilian organizations within its capabilities. SFOR has been routinely extended, and as of March 2002, had some 17,500 troops on the ground. Although U.S. troop contributions to IFOR/SFOR have fallen from 20,000 to around 3,000, the United States still provides the largest national contingent to the force and continues to exercise overall command of SFOR. Despite President George W. Bush's statements that he wants to reduce U.S. troop commitments in the Balkans, most analysts believe NATO troops will likely remain in Bosnia for the foreseeable future.

Has Fighting Ended and Does the State Have Control of the Territory?

Although a peace agreement has been signed and large-scale fighting has come to an end, the Bosnian state makes no pretense of being able to control its territory. The NATO forces do this, and most observers agree that if they leave, fighting will resume very shortly (Bildt 2001; Daalder and Froman 1999; GAO 2000; ICG 2001c).

Have the Combatants Been Disarmed and Demobilized?

Annex 1A of the *General Framework Agreement for Peace* included provisions for a phased program of withdrawing forces to specified zones, the cantonment of all heavy weapons, the confiscation of all personal military equipment (i.e., individual weapons, explosive devices, communications equipment), and the release of personnel from military forces. The agreement also stipulates that the parties were to meet within specified time periods to develop limitations on the size and equipment of the entities' armed forces. However, the agreement allows all three ethnic groups to maintain their own armies, which remain postured against one another. This enhances the risks of renewed conflict as each maintains active intelligence gathering operations and order-of-battle doctrines designed to fight against each other (USIP 2000c).

While all three factions have completed the reduction of their forces to the agreed-upon level of three hundred thousand, the supervised arms reduction program of the Organization for Security and Cooperation in Europe (OSCE) has not been fully complied with, as the Bosnian Serbs have consistently underreported their heavy weapons holdings (Siegel 1998). The Serbs also claim that the U.S.-led "train and equip" program to develop a "national" military capability is designed to give the Bosnian-Croat Federation an unfair advantage over them.

Generally, the major terms of the treaty involving disarmament and demobilization have been implemented, but small groups of armed thugs (paramilitaries) organized and controlled by extremist political leaders continue to operate in the country (GAO 2000).

Have the Basic Structures of the Rule of Law Been (Re)established?

Although the Dayton Accords placed the burden of providing a safe and secure environment on the parties themselves by developing and maintaining civilian law enforcement agencies that operate in accordance with internationally recognized standards, the agreement includes a request that the United Nations deploy an International Police Task Force (IPTF) to assist domestic law enforcement. The civilian police operation, authorized along with IFOR under UNSC Resolution 1035 (1995), was charged with (a) monitoring, observing, and inspecting law enforcement activities and facilities, including associated judicial organizations, structures, and proceedings; (b) advising law enforcement personnel and forces; (c) training law enforcement personnel; (d) facilitating, within the IPTF' s mission of assistance, the parties' law enforcement activities; (e) assessing threats to public order and advising law enforcement agencies on how to deal with such threats; (f) advising governmental authorities in Bosnia and Herzegovina on the organization of effective civilian 1aw enforcement agencies; and (g) accompanying the parties' law enforcement personnel as they carry out their responsibilities, as the IPTF deems appropriate. The agreement also stipulated that the parties must not in any way hinder the work of the IPTF.

Managed by the United Nations Mission in Bosnia-Herzegovina (UN-MIBH), the IPTF was authorized at 1,721 monitors, but did not approach full strength until August 1996. Additionally, many of those who were volunteered by donor countries fell short of the minimal qualifications of fluency in English, the ability to drive, and eight years of experience in policing (as defined in the donor country). Shortages of mission-essential items such as communications equipment, vehicles, and medical care also plagued the IPTF from the beginning (Bair and Dziedzic 1998; Sharp 1997).

Although given a broad mandate, the IPTF was not authorized to carry weapons and relied upon the consent of the parties to carry out its mission. In circumstances where implementation of the accords ran counter to the local interests of one of the parties or when local police refused to cooperate (e.g., the transfer of Serb-held suburbs of Sarajevo to the Bosnian-Croat Federation), an "enforcement gap" arose as the IPTF possessed neither the mandate nor the resources to bring about public order independently (Bair and Dziedzic 1998). Additionally, abuse of ethnic minorities by police officers continued to take place in all three ethnic communities, and some municipal authorities were corrupt and involved in illegal activities. In such cases, the IPTF only was able to conduct limited investigations and implore the appropriate authorities to act in accordance with their own laws, which only had a limited impact (Boutros-Ghali 1997; ICG 2001c).

Because police elements had greatly increased in size during the first half of the 1990s and had carried out much of the ethnic cleansing—the distinction between police and paramilitary forces was blurry—there was a need to reduce the sizes of the forces and to develop a process to screen and clean out those accused of atrocities or deemed unable to play a neutral role in the future. To meet these needs, the IPTF developed a process to certify that all police officers met certain educational prerequisites, underwent a background check showing no history of improper conduct, showed no evidence of psychological disorders, received a passing score on the police knowledge examination, and received the induction training involving an introduction to international standards for policing and human rights. However, a U.S. Government Accounting Office (GAO) report in April 2000 found that many of the local police forces still largely were organized along ethnic lines, continued to resort to excessive force, and at times actively discouraged minority resettlement in majority areas. Additionally, sources have reported that local police have been involved in organizing and leading riots in cases where the Office of the High Representative (OHR) has implemented policies deemed contrary to their "national" interests (ICG 2001c).

While important, police restructuring and training will not prevent a resumption of the conflict and lead to the development of the rule of law in Bosnia. If Bosnia's three nations are to live together within one state, respect for minority rights must become integral to the political and judicial processes. As long as nationalist political leaders command the allegiance of police forces, the public security apparatus will continue to be exploitable as an instrument of repression (Bair and Dziedzic 1998).

Have Refugees Been Repatriated and Internally Displaced People Returned to Their Homes?

As a deliberate strategy by Serbs to ethnically "cleanse" areas under their control during the first half of the 1990s, more than 2.25 million people in Bosnia were displaced by the war (Daalder 1996). While approximately 1.2 million became refugees and were dispersed among twenty-five countries, most of the one million people who became displaced within Bosnia moved to areas controlled by their own ethnic group. As a result, most areas of the country—with the exception of central Bosnia—were populated and controlled by a predominant ethnic group at the end of the war.

Annex 7 of the *General Framework Agreement for Peace* begins by stating that all refugees and displaced persons have the right to return freely to their homes. The annex calls on the parties to the agreement to ensure that all refugees and displaced persons are permitted to return safely, without risk of harassment, intimidation, persecution, or discrimination, particularly on account of their ethnic origin, religious belief, or political opinion.

However, repatriation of refugees and the return of internally displaced persons in Bosnia have proceeded more slowly than hoped by the external actors. Lack of public order and the failure to apprehend war criminals that still exercise much control discouraged many refugees from returning in 1996 and 1997 (Sharp 1997). While some refugees and internally displaced persons do not wish to return to their homes because they enjoy better standards of living in their new communities, many who wish to go home face numerous obstacles. Returning to areas controlled by another ethnic group, these people often face political and legal obstruction such as lack of permits to reconstruct their homes and the inability to secure running water or electricity; in some locations, they have been subject to violent intimidation and sporadic attacks. Local housing officials who seek to comply with laws on returns have also been subject to intimidation and reprisals (Amnesty International 2000). While accurate numbers are hard to come by as many are returning quietly without the assistance of the international community, it is evident that returns have accelerated since 1999, even to the areas in which they are a minority (*Economist* 2000b; OSCE 2001; USIP 2000c).

Recent polling data show that of those refugees and displaced persons who did not wish to return to their prewar homes, 58 percent said the lack of security for themselves and their property is the primary reason they will not return. In contrast, many international officials in Bosnia, including the SFOR commander, believe that, rather than a lack of personal security, the primary obstacle to minority returns is the poor economy, primarily unemployment and a lack of funding to repair homes (GAO 2000).

Whatever the case, political leaders of all three ethnic groups have continued their attempts to maintain (or even take) control of strategically important terrain through the return process. Managing the return of the refugees
and displaced persons is one part of the broader, ongoing struggle in
Bosnia—or to turn Prussian military philosopher Carl Von Clausewitz's famous dictum on its head—a peace that is really the continuation of war by
other means (Daalder 1997; Eyre 2000).

Although the Dayton Accords sought to balance the strategic and tacti-
cal situation among the groups along the entire Inter-Entity Boundary Line,
in certain areas there is competition to gain advantage, and the resettlement
of populations is used by entity governments as a means to ensure their
own military security and is managed as such (Eyre 2000). Bosnian Serbs
have stated repeatedly that they cannot allow Bosnian Croats and Bosnian
Muslims to resettle in the Republika Srpska. Bosnian Croats have prevented Bosnian Serbs from resettling in the western part of the Federation.
Bosnian Muslim authorities have opposed minority returnees in Sarajevo
and Bugojno (Siegal 1998). In one early confrontation, one hundred houses
rebuilt by the international community for minority returnees were burned
only days before they were to be reoccupied (Eyre 2000.) Thus, the return
of refugees and displaced persons cannot be viewed as merely a matter of
accommodating the wishes of the individuals who wish to return.

Have Political Authority and Institutions Been (Re)established in a Manner That Allows the Citizens of the Country to Hold Them Accountable for Their Actions?

While SFOR has ensured an absence of war in Bosnia, political leaders of
the country's three major ethnic groups have continued to obstruct the implementation of the political, humanitarian, and economic provisions of the
Dayton Accords (GAO 2000). Perhaps the greatest obstacle to developing
state authority and institutions is the lack of commitment by the Serbs and
Croats in Bosnia to the political entity. As a minority in the Balkan Region,
Bosnian Muslims seek a strong federal state, while the country's Serbs—and
the Croats to a lesser extent—have sought to weaken the central government
in favor of more local control. Nationalist parties have concentrated their
power at the entity level, and even within the Federation, Muslims and
Croats maintain separate, parallel lines of authority. This has been a major
impediment to the development of more effective governance and the transition to multiethnic democracy (USIP 2000c). Both Serbs and Croats have
professed desires to run their own mini-state or to join Serbia and Croatia
respectively. Again, the Dayton Accords did not end the struggle between the
groups, but diverted the pursuance of that end into different means.

The international community looked to early elections to help establish
common institutions to allow the entities to select representatives who

would work together to implement the Dayton Accords. However, many groups have argued that the early elections—which were held on September 14, 1996—did not allow other groups to organize and instead legitimized the hard-line nationalists who had led the war and who opposed a democratic and multiethnic Bosnia (Sharp 1997).

Under Annex 10 of the Dayton Accords, a "high representative" was to be appointed to facilitate the parties' own efforts and to mobilize and coordinate the activities of the various governmental and nongovernmental organizations involved in the civilian implementation of the agreement. Carl Bildt of Sweden was appointed high representative in December 1995. He was replaced in 1997 by Carl Westendorp of Spain, who was followed by Wolfgang Petritsch of Austria in 1999. At the Peace Implementation Conference held in Bonn, Germany, in December 1997, the major international backers of the Dayton settlement acknowledged numerous problems in the implementation of the agreement, and empowered the high representative to impose binding decisions to overcome the parties' obstructionism and speed up the rebuilding process.

Between 1999 and March 2001, the high representative removed more than twenty officials from their positions for obstructing Dayton implementation, including the elected Bosnian Serb and Bosnian Croat presidents in 1999 and 2001, respectively. The high representative now makes more and more critical decisions for Bosnia, and the burden of implementing Dayton rests more on the international community than the groups within Bosnia (Bildt 2001; Eyre 2000; USIP 2000c).

While advantageous in some respects, giving the high representative wider ranging powers also has had the negative impact of allowing local leaders to abdicate their responsibility for making the difficult decisions that may be unpopular with their constituents in matters such as refugee returns, police reform, and cooperation with the ICTY. This, in turn, reduces political accountability and prolongs the transition from international to true local control (Woodward 1999). Until an organized, effective base committed to the peace process is established within Bosnia that is capable of holding leaders accountable, the ideal of a democratic, multiethnic Bosnia will never take hold.

However, some see signs of hope, as the three leaders who signed the Dayton Accords left office between December 1999 and October 2000. Hardline Croatian President Franjo Tudjman died in December 1999, Bosnian President Alija Izetbegović resigned due to old age in October 2000, and Yugoslav President Slobodan Milošević was pushed from office that same month and has since been turned over to the ICTY, perhaps removing the biggest impediment to peace in the region.

However, while the neighboring countries may be trending toward moderation, nationalists dominated the November 2000 elections within Bosnia. In the Croat-dominated areas of the Federation, hard-line Croats successfully staged a referendum to back their demand to separate themselves from the Muslims and form a separate entity, a move that undermines the premise of the Dayton Accords. It was after Ante Jelavić, the Bosnian Croat member of the three-person presidency, pledged in March 2001 to create a Croat state in Bosnia that the high representative removed him from office.

In the Republika Srpska, the Serbian Democratic Party (SDS) candidate soundly defeated the candidate supported by Dayton proponents. The SDS party was formed by indicted war criminal Radovan Karadžić, who is thought to still wield considerable influence over its affairs. The only bright spot was the strong performance of the multiethnic Social Democratic Party in the federation, which defeated the nationalist Muslim parties.

Is Economic Development Underway?

The Bosnian war had a tremendous impact on the country's economy. For example, at the beginning of 1996, Bosnia's gross national product (GNP) had declined to 10 percent of its prewar size, its per capita income was down to 25 percent, more than 70 percent of the industrial plant had been destroyed, and unemployment stood at 80 percent and was rising as troops were demobilized (Sharp 1997). In addition, the country had to dismantle its centrally planned economic system and create a market-based one in its place.

A $5.1 billion Priority Reconstruction Program for Bosnia was approved in 1996 to finance emergency reconstruction projects and to promote sustainable development by financing small businesses and encouraging foreign investment in the country. IFOR was also active in reconstruction efforts, as military engineers repaired and opened more than 50 percent of the roads in Bosnia and rebuilt more than sixty bridges, including those linking the country with Croatia. They were also involved in de-mining and repairing railroads; opening airports to civilian traffic; restoring gas, water, and electricity supplies; rebuilding schools and hospitals; and restoring key telecommunication assets (Wentz 1998).

Although the country made substantial progress in the years following the Dayton Accords, many of the leading donors—including the World Bank, the International Monetary Fund, the European Union, and individual country donors—tended to work in a bilateral framework, and not as part of a coordinated plan, which prevented greater synergy and hampered the ability to apply pressure on uncooperative parties (Sharp 1997). While the efforts of the external actors have benefited the country, the parties' limited cooperation has slowed down the reconstruction process.

While increasing the stature of central institutions is vital for the development of a multiethnic democracy, it is also necessary for the development of the economy. The central government lacks the ability to develop a national stabilization and structural adjustment program, cohesive regulatory structures, and national banking and transportation structures. Central institutions are also necessary for the ability of the government to develop its own sources of revenue independent of the entities. Presently, the entities (and sometimes sub-entities) control key wealth-producing industries in energy, telecommunications, and transportation. Where privatization has gone forward, it usually has benefited the ruling parties and their patronage networks (USIP 2000c).

After receiving an aid package many times the relative size of the Marshall Plan, Bosnia remains highly dependent upon foreign help. The country's leaders have shown little willingness to commit to the reforms necessary to create a sustainable economy based on a free market. The country has developed a large trade deficit, has virtually no domestic investments, operates under an unsustainable budget dependent upon foreign aid, suffers from massive unemployment, and has inefficient and corrupt institutions (Bildt 2001; USIP 2000c). Instead of lessening their grip on the country's financial sector, privatizing its assets, and creating an atmosphere that encourages private-sector economic activity (including foreign investment), leaders have maintained control of and tolerate, if not participate in, a system rife with corruption—all in the service of what they define to be their nationalist political interests (Daalder and Froman 1999). In July 2000, the U.S. Government Accounting Office (GAO) reported that pervasive crime and corruption were blocking the success of the Dayton peace accord, and that authorities in Bosnia "have not demonstrated a desire to eliminate corruption and develop a society based on the rule of law" (Marquis and Gall 2000). Although the World Bank, the U.S. Agency for International Development (USAID), and the OHR have each done studies and are in general agreement about the nature of the problems and what must be done to resolve them, their recommendations have yet to be implemented (ICG 2001b).

Without fundamental economic and social reforms, desperation among the Bosnian citizens will only grow, feeding nationalist agendas. However, in addition to the major structural issues, Bosnia also suffers from problems that might be better understood as economic opportunism and criminal profiteering than as nationalist conflict. The resistance by some (possibly many) to the implementation of the Dayton Accords is based on their ability to secure financial or political advantage in the current environment (Eyre 2000). For example, checkpoints set up under the guise of promoting local security also allow the police to extract "road taxes" which greatly supplement their low official wages. Another ploy used by forces loyal to Radovan Karadžić is to stop trucks carrying cattle under the pretense of conducting safety inspections. If the trucker intends to take the cattle to a slaughterhouse run by Karadžić's allies, the truck is allowed to pass. If not, the driver is cited for various safety violations and fined an enormous sum on the spot. If the driver cannot produce the cash, the truck and its contents are seized and sent to one of Karadžić's slaughterhouses. The revenue from the contents is then used to pay police salaries and fund Karadžić's political machine (Eyre 2000).

In late July 1999, the European Commission and the World Bank formally established a regional assistance framework called the Stability Pact for South Eastern Europe. The program was intended to coordinate and prioritize economic and other assistance going to the region (which includes all of the former Yugoslav republics except Slovenia, as well as Albania, Bulgaria, and Romania) and to accelerate and deepen the integration of a reformed region into the Euro-Atlantic community. The general idea behind the program was to link regional integration efforts with European ones through the Stabilization and Association Agreements, which provide a flexible structure for eventual integration into Europe. While the Stability Pact held out the hope that, with appropriate reforms, Bosnia and the other countries could eventually join the European market, Bosnia is so far from these goals that it is not likely to get there for decades. The widespread fear is that, in the meantime, despair and cynicism may replace hope, and result in a backlash that leads people more toward embracing nationalist rhetoric.

Additionally, the implicit assumption behind high levels of international aid is that private investment dollars will soon follow. This, however, is not always the case, as the situation in Bosnia suggests to-date (Steil and Woodward 1999). Reports of financial corruption combined with cumbersome Dayton-prescribed institutions have driven away corporate investors. Furthermore, foreign assistance for private enterprise development will be useless unless macroeconomic stability—a clear prerequisite to rational business planning and investment—backs it up.

Has a Mechanism Been Developed to Deal with Past Atrocities and Promote Reconciliation between Groups?

The UN Security Council established the International Criminal Tribunal for the former Yugoslavia (ICTY) in May 1993, two and one-half years before the Dayton Accords were signed. The council created the tribunal to prosecute persons responsible for serious violations of international humanitarian law committed in the territory of the former Yugoslavia since 1991. The tribunal's purpose was to assign guilt for war crimes to individual perpetrators and the leaders responsible, rather than allowing blame to fall on the entire ethnic group or nations. Its founders hoped that the tribunal would thus diffuse ethnic tensions and assist in peacemaking. Established during the war rather than after its conclusion, the founders also hoped it would deter violations for the remainder of the conflict (Meron 1997). Without the establishment of the tribunal, supporters feared that it would send the message to others around the world that they could violate international humanitarian norms with impunity. However, not everyone agreed that a tribunal was the proper path to achieve reconciliation. Critics argued that it would obstruct peace negotiations, making leaders less willing to leave power or agree to provisions that might expose them to prosecution.

The Dayton Accords essentially created three categories of culpability for atrocities committed during the conflict (Kritz 1996). In the first category, the warring parties committed themselves to providing full cooperation and assistance to the ICTY, which sought to prosecute those on each side of the conflict who perpetrated the most heinous offenses (genocide, war crimes, and crimes against humanity). The accords also prohibited any individual indicted by the tribunal from holding public office. In the second category, the agreement obligated the parties to immediately undertake "the prosecution, dismissals, or transfer, as appropriate, of persons in military, paramilitary, and police forces, and other public servants responsible for serious violations of the basic rights of persons belonging to ethnic or minority groups" (Annex 7, Article I). The third category guaranteed amnesty to all returning refugees and displaced persons charged with any crime related to the conflict "other than a serious violation of international humanitarian law" (Annex 7, Article VI).

However, since its inception, the ICTY has been plagued by the lack of co-operation by the parties—especially the Serbs, but also by the Croats to a lesser extent. Indicted criminals have been sheltered and protected, access to sites where atrocities were committed has been obstructed, and witnesses have been pressured to withhold testimony. Because the ICTY has no power to arrest indicted persons, it must rely on the SFOR troops and/or local leaders to do so. Fearing that the attempt to arrest war criminals would result in casualties (which would undermine international support for the overall mission) and claiming that the task is more of a "policing" than a "military" function, SFOR has adopted the position that it will detain indictees if they come across them, but that it will not pursue them (Sharp 1997). Although the British forces have been somewhat more aggressive in arresting those indicted, U.S. and French forces have been more cautious. Local leaders, on the other hand, have few incentives to do so, especially because of the well-entrenched networks of support some of the more prominent indictees have. Radovan Karadžić, the Bosnian Serb political leader in the early 1990s, and Radko Mladić, the Bosnian Serb military leader, both remain at large. Richard Holbrooke (2001), the chief negotiator behind the Dayton Accords, has stated that the reluctance of NATO to arrest Karadžić and Mladić is the single thing that has most distressed him about Western policy since the agreement in 1995. Holbrooke argued that the arrests would make the Dayton Accords much more effective, and would allow the peacekeepers to be withdrawn more quickly.

In recent years, partly due to the limited ability of the ICTY to bring indicted criminals to trial, and partly due to the logistical problem that many of the people involved in crimes simply cannot be held accountable by the international court, some have looked to the establishment of a "truth commission" as a complement to the ICTY. Suggestions have been made to pattern a multiethnic commission along the lines of the Truth and Reconciliation Commission in South Africa, where national reconciliation is brought about through a public airing of the atrocities and where those who testify may be granted amnesties or pardons. Concerns are voiced that unless there is a greater sense of justice, the Bosnian reconciliation process cannot get very far. Such a commission would facilitate the development of a credible and more unified historical understanding of the Bosnian wars, thereby helping replace the biased group histories that can foment new conflict (USIP 2000b).

Have Efforts Been Made to (Re)establish Local Governance, Encourage the Development of Civil Society, and Promote Community-Building Activities in General?

Numerous governmental and nongovernmental organizations have promoted initiatives that seek to strengthen local accountability and civil society, while reducing ethnic tensions among the societal groups. An interreligious council has been formed to encourage citizens to work together to replace hostility with cooperation and respect, and to acknowledge their shared moral commitment to peace and reconciliation. However, the concentration of power at the entity level has impeded the development of effective governance at the cantonal and municipal levels (USIP 2000c).

The U.S. Agency for International Development's (USAID) Office of Transition Initiatives (OTI) began operating in Bosnia immediately after the signing of the Dayton Accords as part of the larger U.S. government effort to assist in postconflict reconciliation and reconstruction. The goals of OTI were to (1) reshape hard-line nationalist attitudes; (2) promote respect for the democratic processes, human rights, and basic freedoms; (3) disseminate more objective information; and (4) effect positive political change (OTI 2000b). OTI initially focused on working through civil society organizations, but shifted to electronic and print media after an April 1999 review of the program. The general goal has been to support media outlets that are not under the control of hard-line nationalists in order to allow diverse, more moderate, and objective voices to be heard.

Do Citizens Support Belonging to the Entity?

The vast majority of Bosnian Serbs and Bosnian Croats do not support the current political structure in Bosnia and seek either independent states or ones joined with Serbia and Croatia, respectively. On the other hand, most Bosnian Muslims support a unified, multiethnic Bosnia, and see themselves as the rightful leaders of that entity (GAO 2000). Most Muslims believe a partition of the country would leave them vulnerable to more dominant powers in the region. External actors seek to maintain a unified Bosnia, fearing that partition would create a more unstable environment in the region and set a dangerous precedent that it is acceptable to establish ethnicity as the basis for a state (Talbott 1999). Both the Bosnian Muslims and the external actors see returnees as the potential glue that will hold Bosnia together, arguing that minorities will feel more secure in a multiethnic unit than one in which they have little or no say (USIP 2000c).

SUMMARY AND CONCLUSIONS

As the state of Yugoslavia began breaking up in 1990, the Muslims in the Bosnian Republic found themselves in a tug of war between the more powerful and more dominant Serb and Croat states and peoples. After Croatia declared its independence from Yugoslavia in 1991, Bosnia felt it had little choice but to declare its independence as well. The Serbs, who comprised only about a third of the Bosnian people, quickly and effectively—yet brutally—grabbed as much land in Bosnia as they could with the hope that they could join Serbia. In "ethnically cleansing" the countryside and indiscriminately shelling major cities, the Serbs became viewed by the international community as the perpetrators of the conflict.

Although several diplomatic agreements were put forth, none took hold until the international community developed a common approach toward the region, NATO forces undertook systematic and extensive air raids against Serbian targets in Bosnia, and Croatian forces began expelling Serbs from the Krajina Region in Croatia. After signing a cease-fire in October 1995, the leaders of Serbia, Croatia, and Bosnia met in Dayton, Ohio, and agreed to a comprehensive peace plan that was formally signed in December 1995.

However, after more than five years of a NATO military presence and high levels of international assistance and attention, many of the fundamental problems remain. Bosnia is an artificial state, held together by an international military presence and internationally-defined sovereign borders. While daily life in Bosnia has improved from the war-ravaged society it was during the first half of the 1990s, the former warring parties largely retain their wartime goals, and, according to many observers, would resume war if the NATO-led troops were withdrawn. Instead of moving toward self-sustaining peace and economic growth as envisioned under the Dayton Accords, the country's economy, politics, and even its security remain firmly dependent upon foreign, rather than Bosnian, efforts.

In short, the Bosnian state is not capable of performing any of the three tasks set out as necessary in chapter 1. It is not capable of exercising its authority and providing security to its citizens, it is not able to effectively resolve conflicts through its institutions or promote the general welfare of its citizens, and it is not viewed as legitimate by those who live under it. Although the international community has provided many of these functions for the citizens of Bosnia, it has not enabled the Bosnian state to develop the capacity to provide them on its own. If external actors are to rectify the situation so that they are able to leave a capable, effective, and legitimate Bosnian state, they must better target the areas that are essential to state development and ensure that they are working to create Bosnian entities that will be able to assume those tasks.

By and large, the overall framework of the Dayton peace agreement is sound, although some provisions that impede greater integration may need to be renegotiated (which is easier said than done). For example, some mechanism must be developed to demobilize the three separate armies that currently exist in Bosnia, and create one national force in its place. While it may have been necessary to allow them to remain in the immediate post-Dayton period, they should be phased out in a manner that does not create vulnerability for any group. Not only does the current system draw substantial resources from an impoverished country, but it also reinforces the ethnic boundaries and suspicions of each group. While it may not be necessary to eliminate all forces in each region, they must be reduced to a much lower level and clearly subordinated to a national authority.

Additionally, much more emphasis needs to be directed at developing a police force that can both provide security to all citizens and work to eliminate corruption. The current police force is more a part of the problem than part of any solution. While the IPTF has done some good work, the mandate must be much broader and have more teeth. Requirements to create such a force go beyond training, and must include removing officers who are unable to perform their work in a neutral manner, as well as removing the reasons that promote or facilitate the corruption. Such a force must also work toward removing both formal and informal impediments to refugee and displaced person returns. Finally, the persons indicted by the ICTY must be arrested and brought to trial so that they are prevented from exercising (usually informal) authority within the country and to promote a sense of justice among the citizens.

The most difficult task of all is to create political will among the domestic parties to promote a peaceful, multiethnic polity. Many of the leaders have risen to power on nationalist agendas and fear they will lose support if they cooperate with the Dayton process. While it is beyond the abilities of the external actors to create the political will, they can facilitate it by supporting moderate leaders who are willing to lead their people down its path. While the power-sharing arrangements included in Dayton were designed in the climate of war, some may need to be modified to allow a transition to a more mature relationship among the groups. For example, Sharp (1997) has advocated a change in the voting process for president that would give a citizen three votes (one for each ethnic group) rather than a single vote for one's own ethnic group. Her argument is that this change in the system would encourage candidates to reach across ethnic lines to develop support rather than just play to the hard-line nationalist elements within one's own group. Additionally, laws must be developed and enforced across the state that are capable of regulating economic and other governmental activities that can allow the development of private enterprise and reduce corruption.

One cannot be naïve about the depth of the hostility and distrust among the ethnic groups in Bosnia, and it will not be easy to overcome the abuses committed in their names, especially when the conflict was so recent and so devastating. And while the external actors also are unable to create a legitimate government for the citizens of Bosnia, again, they may be able to facilitate the process. External actors can support domestic efforts to add a truth and reconciliation-type commission to the work of the ICTY in attempting to promote healing within communities and create a greater awareness of the victims on each side of the conflict. Additionally, while the means for fostering civil society and building a robust, participatory, and inclusive governance process are far from clear, external actors can support the work of local NGOs that are working towards those ends and support efforts to meet the health and educational needs of the Bosnian people. When a government is seen to be effective at meeting basic needs, it is likely to enjoy more support of the people.

NOTE

1. Although the proper name for the country under discussion in this chapter is Bosnia and Herzegovina, the term Bosnia is used for simplicity.

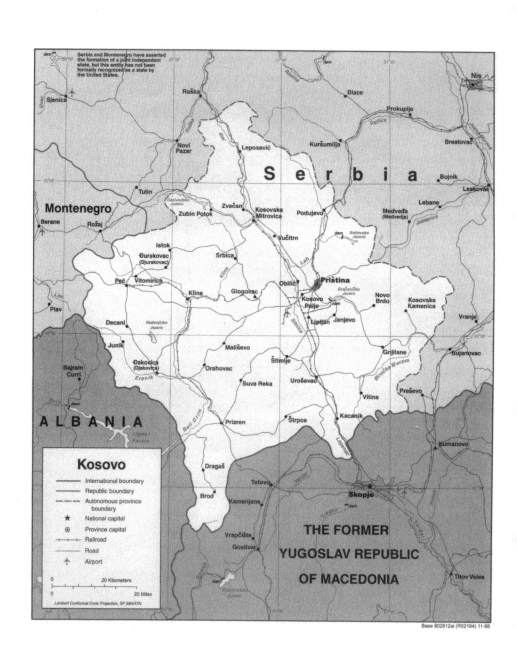

Serbia and Montenegro have asserted the formation of a joint independent state, but this entity has not been formally recognized as a state by the United States.

Nis

Sjenica

Raška

Blace

Prokuplje

Brestovac

Novi Pazar

Leposavić

Kuršumlija

S e r b i a

Bojnik

Tutin

Leskovac

Montenegro

Zvečan

Kosovska Mitrovica

Podujevo

Lebane

Medveđa (Medvedja)

Berane

Rožaj

Zubin Potok

Vučitrn

Istok

Đurakovac (Djurakovac)

Srbica

Peć

Vitomirica

Klina

Glogovac

Obilić

Priština

Novo Brdo

Kosovska Kamenica

Decani

Kosovo Polje

Lipljan

Janjevo

Vranje

Junik

Mališevo

Gnjilane

Bujanovac

Bajram Curri

Đakovica (Djakovica)

Orahovac

Štimlje

Uroševac

Vitina

Preševo

Suva Reka

A L B A N I A

Prizren

Štrpce

Kacanik

Kumanovo

Dragaš

Tetovo

Brod

Kamenjane

Skopje

Vrapčište

Gostivar

THE FORMER

YUGOSLAV REPUBLIC

OF MACEDONIA

Titov Veles

Kosovo

International boundary
Republic boundary
Autonomous province boundary
★ National capital
◉ Province capital
Railroad
Road
✈ Airport

0   20 Kilometers
0   20 Miles

Lambert Conformal Conic Projection, SP 38N/47N

Base 802612ai (R02194) 11-98

CHAPTER 5

KOSOVO

"The Yugoslav crisis began in Kosovo,[1] and it will end in Kosovo," is a phrase one might hear almost anywhere in the former Yugoslavia. However, no one is quite sure how—or when—the crisis will end. Although a seventy-eight-day bombing campaign in 1999 ended with an agreement on the principles upon which a final solution to the status of the separatist province would be based, no timetable has been set for its final resolution.

On a basic level, the conflict over Kosovo appears to be an "ethnic" one. After all, the controversy is largely between Albanians and Serbs who are of different ancestral groups, different religious traditions, and speak different languages. The Albanians form an overwhelming majority in the province, but a relatively small minority in all of Serbia. However, once one probes beneath the surface and considers the true history and the political machinations of the last century—rather than the "myths" that form current lore—the notion of the conflict emanating from ancient ethnic and religious hatreds is less convincing.

BACKGROUND OF THE CONFLICT

Serb roots in the Balkan Region can be traced back to the sixth and seventh centuries. However, Serbs did not exert control over the entire region or even continuously occupy a certain territory. Two rival theories exist that identify Albanian roots as either with the Illyrians (who lived in the western half of the Balkans from pre-Roman times) or the Thracians (who lived in the eastern portion of the Balkans). Albanian historians, who like the idea that their ancestors have always lived in Albania, prefer the Illyrian theory, while many other scholars put them on the Thracian side (Malcolm 1998).

With borders continually in flux—as was common in medieval Europe—the Serbian Kingdom never had an official capital, and dominant centers of royal residence and administration tended to shift with changes in rulers. Prince Lazar, the ruler with whom much of the Serb claim to Kosovo rests, had his center of administration inside present-day Serbia, but well north of the current borders of the province of Kosovo. Although a number of Orthodox churches and monasteries were built in what is present-day Kosovo, the city of Peć likely became the seat of the archbishopric and then the patriarchate of the Serbian church because of an attack on the monastery of Žiča (near Lazar's administrative center) in 1290 by marauding bands (Malcolm 1998).

The Ottoman Turks began to wrest control of the Balkans away from local rulers in the late fourteenth century. As the Serbian Kingdom had weakened after the death of Tsar Dušan in 1355, there were numerous battles in the region between the Serbs and Ottomans, but none have taken on as much significance as the Battle of Kosovo in 1389. Serb lore has it that St. Ilija (Elijah) appeared to Prince Lazar before the battle (in the form of a falcon) and offered him a choice between an earthly kingdom and a heavenly one. Lazar chose the heavenly one, saying that "it is better to die in battle that to live in shame." Because of this decision, described as a "covenant with God," the Serbs are often said to consider themselves a "heavenly people" (Malcolm 1998, 80). The Serbs lost the battle (in which Prince Lazar was killed), but they claim that the effort wore down the Ottomans and stalled their onslaught, saving Europe from the Muslims.

Despite the fact that historical accounts of the battle are somewhat different than the myth, the evidence of history has not shaken the widespread Serbian conviction, derived from the Battle of Kosovo, that Europe owes the Serbs special treatment (Zimmerman 1999). However, there is no evidence of Serbs drawing significance from this battle or the notion of a special "covenant" between Lazar and God until the nineteenth century, when nationalists began promoting the idea that the medieval battle was a defining political event in the history of the Serb people (Malcolm 1998).[2]

Throughout the next five centuries, the Ottomans controlled the entire Balkan Region. While the Orthodox Serbs refused to convert to Islam, the Albanians (as had the Bosnians) generally did convert in order to enhance their position among local rivals. In 1689, Serbs in the area of present-day Kosovo revolted against Ottoman rule. After the revolt failed, many Serbs fled the region to seek safety in southern Hungary. This exodus started the trend toward Albanian dominance in the province.

After putting down a series of revolts in the early 1800s, the Ottoman sultan agreed to allow Serbia to exercise extensive powers of self-administration under its own prince in 1815, although it would remain under Ottoman sovereignty. With growing restiveness under eroding Ottoman rule, Russia declared war on Istanbul in 1877, hoping to secure territorial assets in the region. As a result of treaties ending the war in 1878, Bosnia was ceded to Austro-Hungary, Serbia became a fully independent state, and Kosovo remained a part of the territories ruled by the Ottomans. However, because part of Kosovo's territory had been given to Montenegro, widespread resentment grew within Kosovo against the treaty and sparked resistance that would help contribute to the downfall of the Ottoman Empire thirty-four years later (Malcolm 1998).

Even before its independence, Serbia had tried to seize Kosovo in what was known as the "Eastern Crisis" of 1875–1878, but was repelled by Albanian nationalists living there. During the Balkan War of 1912, however, Serbia did succeed in conquering and annexing Kosovo. During the attack, Slavic Christians (mainly Serbs and Montenegrins) massacred or expelled many of the province's Ottoman Turkish elites, as well as Muslim Albanians. More Muslims were killed during and in the aftermath of World War I, as the Serb government attempted to settle its people in the area and to "Serbianize" the Albanian majority linguistically and politically (Hagen 1999). In the Kingdom of Serbs, Croats, and Slovenes created after the war, Kosovo was essentially a colony of the state's Serb component.

During World War II, Kosovo was taken from Serbia by the Nazis and joined to Albania (which had been an Italian colony since 1939). The Kosovars were encouraged to fight against the Serbs and Tito's communist "Partisans," and Albanians working for the Nazis carried out many atrocities against Serbs (as also occurred in pro-Nazi Croatia). After World War II, Kosovo was pulled back into the Yugoslav state (after fighting it for a year) and was ruled in a semicolonial fashion by Serbia, leading to the exodus of many Albanians, although those that remained still constituted a majority of Kosovo's residents. In 1961, Albanians comprised about 67 percent of the province's population, the Serbs about 25 percent (Woodward 1995). Poor economic conditions led to violent demonstrations in the late 1960s and early 1970s, leading Tito to grant the province wide-ranging autonomy. This autonomy increased anxieties among Serbs in the region and many migrated out of the province, leaving Kosovo even more heavily Albanian. By 1991, Albanians comprised about 90 percent of Kosovo's population (Woodward 1995).

In 1981, demonstrations by Albanian students against the working and living conditions in Kosovo turned bloody, accelerating the exit of Serbs and Montenegrins. In another of the competing "myths" contrasting the Serb and Albanian views of Kosovo's history, most Serbs saw the protests as inspired by Albanian-backed Islamic fundamentalists seeking to tear Kosovo away from Serbia. On the other hand, most Kosovar Albanians saw the strikes as attempts to highlight legitimate grievances. However, they claim that Serb nationalists seized upon the strikes in order to give Belgrade a pretext to crackdown on the Kosovar Albanians (Mertus 1999).

After rising to the position of president of the Republic of Serbia in 1986, Slobodan Milošević found that trampling on Albanian rights was almost universally popular with Serbs, and not just those with a limited grasp of political issues. According to Warren Zimmerman (1999, 25), the U.S. ambassador to Yugoslavia from 1989 to 1992 (he also served in the country as a foreign service officer in the late 1960s), Milošević was an opportunist rather than an ideologue, a man driven by power rather than nationalism, and a man who "calculated that the way to achieve and maintain power in Serbia was to seize the nationalist pot that Serbian intellectuals were brewing and bring it to a boil."

In June 1989, Milošević gave his now-famous speech at a commemoration of the 600th anniversary of the Battle of Kosovo, revoking the province's autonomy and reintroducing direct rule from Belgrade. In attempting to "re-Serbianize" the public sphere of Kosovo, many Albanian public workers were fired from their jobs (which were then given to Serbs) and schools were ordered to conduct classes in Serbo-Croatian rather than Albanian. Although there was some violence, the majority of the Albanians reacted by following the ideology of nonviolent nationalist separation espoused by their political leader, Ibrahim Rugova. A soft-spoken, yet determined man, Rugova patterned his actions on those of Mahatma Gandhi who rid India of British rule four decades earlier. This strategy entailed forming a parallel public sector in which Albanians would run their own tax system, schools, legal and police organs alongside the "Serbianized" ones.

In early 1990, Rugova and many other Kosovar Albanians expressed the belief that Kosovo should be autonomous within a confederal Yugoslavia. However, by the end of the year, that attitude had changed to the idea of either an independent Kosovar state or one linked to Albania. In the wake of the secession of Slovenia and Croatia from the Federal Republic of Yugoslavia, Kosovo's Albanian majority voted to secede from the state, and indicated a desire to merge with Albania. However, Yugoslavia did not accept Kosovar independence. As Serb actions in the province became more forceful, U.S. President George Bush warned Belgrade in late 1991 that the United States would use force if the Serbs attacked the Kosovo Albanians.

Although Rugova held his followers steadfast in their resistance to Serb rule, they remained largely peaceful in their protests. Over the next four years, most attention—both locally and internationally—was focused on the conflicts between the Serbs, Croats, and Bosnians. However, the 1995 Dayton Accords may have ended the Bosnian war, but it adversely affected the struggle between the Kosovars and Serbs. The agreement called on the European Union (EU) to recognize the Federal Republic of Yugoslavia (now comprised of Serbia and Montenegro), something it earlier had said it would not do until the Kosovo issue was resolved. Many Kosovars felt betrayed by this act, which removed international leverage they had relied upon to secure their freedom from Serb rule. It also lent credence to the arguments of younger, more militant Albanians who advocated violent means as the only way to get attention and respect, and who moved many away from attempting to peacefully protest and negotiate their differences.

With anarchy in Albania and arms easily available, in 1997 the Kosovo Liberation Army (KLA),[3] a small militant group, began killing Serb policemen and collaborators. They also established areas from which the Serbs were driven away entirely. Hashim Thaci, one of the KLA commanders, later said that (because of the Dayton Accords) he decided that only through armed struggle could Kosovo be liberated from its Serb occupiers (Sell 2001).

Using KLA activities as justification, Milošević launched a brutal offensive against Kosovo in 1998 in an attempt to wipe out the militants. In the process, more than fifteen hundred Kosovar civilians were killed and abused, villages were burned, and about three hundred thousand ethnic Albanians were forced from their homes (Daalder and O'Hanlon 2000; NATO 1999). The United States and European countries put forward numerous diplomatic initiatives to deal with the growing crisis, but Milošević agreed to none of them.

EFFORTS BY EXTERNAL ACTORS

Following the rapid deterioration of the situation in the early fall, the North Atlantic Council (the political decision-making body of NATO) authorized air strikes on October 13, 1998. This move was designed to support diplomatic efforts to make the Milošević regime withdraw forces from Kosovo, cooperate in bringing an end to the violence, and facilitate the return of refugees to their homes (NATO 1999). At the last moment, President Milošević agreed to comply with international demands to withdraw troops, facilitate the return of refugees, and accept eighteen hundred unarmed international (OSCE) monitors, and the air strikes were called off. While the agreement had humanitarian benefits because it allowed refugees to return to their homes before winter set in, the lack of an international security presence also allowed KLA rebels to move into the security vacuum (Daalder and O'Hanlon 2000).

After dozens of ethnic Albanians were slain by Serb forces and paramilitary groups during January 1999, international officials demanded a war crimes investigation and insisted that the warring sides attend a peace conference in Rambouillet, France. After initially rejecting the plan presented to parties at the conference, the Kosovars eventually agreed to sign a peace deal calling for the withdrawal of all Serb military forces (with the exception of twenty-five hundred border guards), broad interim autonomy, twenty-eight thousand NATO troops to implement the peace plan, and a diplomatic process to craft a final resolution after three years. While the Serb government expressed a willingness to grant some autonomy to the province, it was adamantly opposed to the deployment of NATO troops and determining a final settlement in three years, fearing the process might well lead to Kosovar independence. Correspondingly, the Serb Parliament solidly rejected the plan. While a number of authors (Daalder and O'Hanlon 2000; Hagen 1999; Judah 2000; Posen 2000) have speculated on Serb rationale for not consenting to the agreement, most support the idea that Milošević probably gambled that he could withstand a period of air strikes, that the inevitable collateral damage would weaken international support for the conflict, and that Russia would raise the costs of the war for the Western powers in the process, weakening the cohesion of the NATO alliance, all of which would allow the Serbs to come away with some deal more favorable than Rambouillet.

When NATO air strikes began in late March 1999, Milošević immediately implemented a planned campaign of ethnic cleansing of Kosovo, hoping to present a fait accompli to the external actors. Within weeks, Serb troops and paramilitary groups forced nearly half of the 1.8 million ethnic Albanians living in Kosovo from their homes. However, the wholesale expulsions during the early part of the war, coupled with refugee accounts of large-scale Serb brutality, probably helped cement Western support for the international effort (Posen 2000).

The accidental bombings of the Chinese embassy and Albanian refugees in the village of Korisa in early May likely prompted Milošević to continue to hold out, hoping the collateral damage would exacerbate differences between the NATO countries and prompt them to negotiate some way out of the conflict. Although bombings against downtown Belgrade were suspended temporarily for a period after the Chinese embassy was hit, NATO stepped up the attacks in mid-May and began systematic destruction of key power transmission installations in the Serbian electric grid (Posen 2000). As intransigence grew on each side as the weeks passed—both sides had expected some deal to be reached within a short period of time—the International Criminal Tribunal for the former Yugoslavia (ICTY), which had begun its work almost two years earlier in the context of the Bosnian conflict, indicted Milošević and four other Serbian leaders for crimes against humanity and related charges.

By the end of May, Milošević probably realized he was not going to achieve much more by holding out any longer and, under pressure from Russia, agreed to a set of principles developed by the Group of 8 (G-8).[4] The largest sticking point in the ensuing discussions had to do with how significant a role the United Nations would play in the settlement versus that of NATO (Posen 2000). The eventual agreement included all of NATO's critical demands: the end of violence, the withdrawal of all Serb security forces from Kosovo, the deployment of a substantial and unconstrained NATO force in Kosovo, the return of refugees, and a commitment from Yugoslavia to "substantial self-government for Kosovo."

From the Russian and Serb points of view, the document included a number of advantages over the Rambouillet Accords: (1) a central political role for the United Nations (rather than NATO) in the "interim" administration of the province (allowing Russia and China to exert more influence over affairs), (2) an acknowledgement that "self-government" must also take into consideration the "sovereignty and territorial integrity of the Federal Republic of Yugoslavia," (3) the presence of Russian troops in the security forces that would deploy in Kosovo, (4) the demilitarization of the KLA, and (5) no explicit reference to any process that could lead to de jure independence for Kosovo. The three-year timetable for a final settlement was replaced with a more ambiguous clause that declared, "the international civil and security presences are established for an initial period of twelve months, to continue thereafter until the Security Council decides otherwise" (Posen 2000). Milošević and the Serb Parliament accepted the agreement on June 3, bringing an effective end to the military conflict.

On June 10, 1999, the UN Security Council adopted Resolution 1244 calling for the deployment of an international security force and the establishment of a civilian UN mission to serve as the interim government for Kosovo. The security force authorized under Chapter VII of the UN Charter was to include "substantial North Atlantic Treaty Organization participation . . . deployed under unified command and control" arrangements. The force was designed to deter renewed hostilities; maintain and, where necessary, enforce a cease-fire; ensure the withdrawal of Serbian forces; and demilitarize the KLA and other armed Albanian groups. The Kosovo Force—or KFOR as it was called—also was charged with establishing a secure environment in which refugees and displaced persons could return home safely, the international civil presence could operate, a transitional administration could be developed, and humanitarian aid could be delivered. Additionally, KFOR was asked to ensure public safety and order until an international police force could take responsibility for this task.

The UN Interim Administration Mission in Kosovo (UNMIK), the civilian portion of the mandate, was essentially given authority over the territory and people of Kosovo. UNMIK's responsibilities were to perform basic civilian administrative functions, promote the establishment of substantial autonomy within the Federal Republic of Yugoslavia (FRY) and providing self-government in Kosovo, and facilitate a political process to determine Kosovo's future status. UNMIK also sought to coordinate humanitarian and disaster relief from all international agencies, support the reconstruction of key infrastructure, maintain civil law and order, promote human rights, and assure the safe and unimpeded return of all refugees and displaced persons to their homes in Kosovo. UNMIK was to be headed by the Special Representative of the Secretary General (SRSG), who would preside over the four "pillars" in Kosovo's reconstruction and facilitate the political process designed to determine Kosovo's future status.

The four pillars were an innovative arrangement designed to divide the tasks among international organizations with resources and expertise in the area. The original Pillar I was led by the United Nations Office of the High Commissioner for Refugees (UNHCR) and was responsible for organizing and implementing humanitarian assistance and refugee repatriation. However, this task focused on the emergency stage of UNMIK's operations and was phased out at the end of June 2000. In May 2001, a new Pillar I was established which focused on police and justice issues, and is under the leadership of the United Nations. Pillar II deals with civil administration and also is led by the United Nations. Pillar III handles democratization and institutionbuilding and is under the direction of the Organization for Security and Cooperation in Europe (OSCE). Pillar IV is charged with the reconstruction and economic development efforts and is managed by the European Union (EU). Michael Steiner, a German, took over the role of SRSG in February 2002. He succeeded Hans Haekkerup of Denmark who had taken over for Dr. Bernard Kouchner of France, the first international administrator of the province.

EVALUATION OF EXTERNAL EFFORTS

The external intervention was undoubtedly successful in diffusing the humanitarian emergency in the short term. While one can argue that the air strikes initially prompted a far worse humanitarian situation than had previously existed, the Serb security forces had conducted numerous raids that left hundreds of Albanians dead and hundreds of thousands uprooted in the previous few months, with little reason to expect anything but a worsening of the situation. Between January 1998 and May 1999, a total of 1.5 million of the 1.8 million ethnic Albanian residents of Kosovo were displaced, with almost half fleeing across an international border (USAID 1999). While efforts to assist the Kosovar refugees and internally displaced persons started long before the air war of early 1999, it kicked into high gear at the conclusion of the eleven-week NATO air campaign.

The international relief effort was coordinated by UNHCR, and assisted by hundreds of governmental and nongovernmental groups. Because the world had watched and read the stories of refugees massing on the borders of Albania and Macedonia and heard stories of Serb atrocities, humanitarian agencies found themselves in the unusual circumstance of having funds pressed upon them by international donors rather than having to beg for funds. Food, water, temporary shelter, and basic health needs were provided, and plans were developed to assist the refugees' longer-term needs, including more permanent shelter to withstand the upcoming winter. Because most crops had not been planted and much livestock destroyed or dispersed, the

Kosovars were dependent upon international food supplies. Additionally, external actors helped Kosovars to mark and remove land mines and unexploded ordnance, and attempt to restore basic services such as electricity and water.

As with Bosnia, the answer to the question of whether external intervention has laid the foundation for the development of a capable, effective, and legitimate state that could avert a relapse into violence is more complicated. However, the most difficult issue facing Kosovo is the province's future status.

Has an Agreement Been Signed to End the Conflict?

While the agreement to end the NATO air strikes set out a series of principles upon which the political solution to the Kosovo crisis was to be determined, it left open the ultimate status of the province. It provided for substantial autonomy for the region, but was to take "full account of the Rambouillet accords and the principles of sovereignty and territorial integrity of the Federal Republic of Yugoslavia." A nationalist Serb can understand the clause to mean that adhering to the principles of sovereignty and territorial integrity means that there will be no independent Kosovo. On the other hand, a pro-independence Kosovar can construe this to mean that the political future in Kosovo is dependent upon a vote of the people within the province (as provided for in the Rambouillet Accords) or through following procedures set out in the Helsinki Final Act, which does not preclude a peaceful change of borders.

There are essentially seven—not necessarily exclusive—options to resolve Kosovo's status in the future. First, Kosovo could remain a part of the FRY, either as an autonomous province or as a third Republic with equal status to that of Serbia and Montenegro. The majority of the Serbs support this position, while almost all Kosovars see it as unacceptable. This option has the de facto support of the international community, at least in the interim, fearing any other option would lead to greater destabilization in the region. If Kosovo is to remain a part of the FRY indefinitely, however, most recognize that this would necessitate a long-term international presence to allow wounds to heal, and would most likely have to be imposed by force on recalcitrant Kosovars, who would likely resort to guerrilla tactics against international forces they would regard as occupiers (Sell 2001).

Second, Kosovo could become an independent state. Having tasted de facto independence, virtually all Albanians would be willing to fight to prevent anything that smacked of a return of Belgrade's rule to the province (ICG 2002a; Sell 2001). Indeed, many Kosovars claim that Belgrade's record since 1989 deprives it of any moral or legal right to rule Kosovo. While independence is fiercely opposed by most Serbs, many in the international community fear that secession would "give heart to separatists and irredentists of every stripe elsewhere in the region" and would undermine any hopes for multiethnic societies in Bosnia or Macedonia (Talbott 1999). Russia and China, each having their own concerns about the precedent of a minority region seceding and being granted independence, will likely insist that any final status resolution has Belgrade's approval (ICG 2002a).

Conditional independence is a third option (ICG 2002a; IICK 2000). This option would end the FRY's sovereignty over Kosovo, yet recognize that the province is not prepared for outright independence. Under what would be tantamount to an international trusteeship, Kosovo would be given enhanced self-government, but would be subject to international oversight until such time the international community deemed the territory able to manage its own affairs. During such time, an international security force would remain in place for external security while a domestic police force continues to gradually assume authority for internal security. While having the benefits of ensuring that the rights of minorities are protected and allowing a long-term economic policy framework to be developed in the meantime, this option commits the international community to an open-ended engagement and may spark fears in other states over a new form of colonialism and restrictions on sovereignty.

A fourth option is to unite the province with the country of Albania. While this possibility received a fair amount of discussion in 1999, it largely has been dropped from serious consideration. NATO and many regional governments fear that this route would undermine Macedonia (which is 25 percent ethnic Albanian) and rekindle ideas of creating a "Greater Albania" (which has no more appeal to external actors than a "Greater Serbia"). Additionally, many Kosovar Albanians do not want to be junior partners in a state that has had the lowest standard of living in all of Europe.

Fifth, Kosovo could be partitioned. There are numerous ways this could be done, but the most widely discussed option is to partition Kosovo along the Ibar River with north going to Serbia, and the rest remaining in the hands of the Albanians, either as an independent country or joined with Albania. This would be technically easy to arrange since, on a practical level, Kosovo is already partitioned in this manner with most Serbs living in the northern region and NATO guarding the pockets of Serbs in the southern areas. However, the Trepca mining complex, deemed important to both communities for political as well as economic reasons, is located north of the Ibar River (ICG 2002a). Additionally, few of the religious or historical sites sacred to Serb memory lie in the northern part, and the international community would be forced to swallow words about multinational states and rights of return. In negotiating partition, Kosovo also almost certainly would seek the Presevo Valley region in southern Serbia, largely inhabited by Albanians, in exchange for the northern region. Any such border change might again increase pressure for Albanians in Macedonia to separate and join the Albanian state (Sell 2001).

A sixth option may be to form a loose, time-limited (perhaps five-year) confederation of Serbia, Montenegro, and Kosovo that would buy time until a permanent solution could be negotiated. Under such an arrangement, Serbia, Montenegro, and Kosovo would have complete legislative, executive, and judicial control over their own internal affairs, and would be required to allow minorities within their borders to exercise full human rights and control over their own local affairs, including police, education, social welfare, and the like. Pending a decision on final status, a strong international civilian and military presence would remain in Kosovo, and before a member could withdraw after the stipulated time period, it would be required to negotiate, under international supervision, guarantees of stable and friendly relations with all neighboring states, renunciation of any territorial changes, respect for minorities, and guarantees for the free flow of peoples, commerce, and information with neighboring states (Sell 2001).

The final option would be to embed an independent Kosovo in a web of economic, political, and security relationships either with Serbia, Montenegro, Bosnia, and Macedonia (Sell 2001) or with all the former Yugoslav states as well as Albania, Romania, Bulgaria, Greece and perhaps the European part of Turkey (Galtung and Mushakoji 1999). The most important element of this regional association or commonwealth would be a single economic zone in which people, goods, labor, and capital could move freely among all the participating states. It also would have to include political and security agreements (possibly under OSCE provisions for regional cooperation), incorporate assurances for the respect of sovereignty and territorial integrity, ensure access to religious and cultural monuments, and promote contacts between minority groups and their "home" state, as well as include arms-control provisions.

Deliberations on Kosovo's final status also have been affected by a number of recent occurrences. First, in October 2000, Milošević was pushed from power in Yugoslavia. As long as Milošević remained president, it was unlikely that external actors were going to return Kosovo to Serbian control, and many saw it as inevitable that Kosovo would eventually become independent. The election of Vojislav Kostunića has rekindled hope that some sort of federal arrangement may be workable. However, Kosovar Albanians argue it is not important who runs Serbia, claiming that all Serbs are nationalists and, even if the present leaders in Belgrade agree to allow the province substantial autonomy, there is no guarantee that a leader in the future may not revoke it.

Second, Montenegro is openly discussing declaring its independence from what is left of Yugoslavia. If Montenegro becomes independent, Kosovo probably also will resist maintaining ties with Belgrade. However, if Montenegro opts for some type of association, pressure will increase on Kosovo to do the same. Third, conflict has erupted in neighboring Macedonia where ethnic Albanians are calling for an increased role over their affairs in that state or even independence. Some see this violence as a prelude to an attempt to secede from the country and join Kosovo if given independence.

Has Fighting Ended and Does the State Have Control of the Territory?

Although KFOR's presence has ended any external threat to Kosovo, there is no domestic force that is capable of providing security for the province and that task will fall on external actors for years to come. While some extremist groups still exist and it is likely that weapons have been hidden around the province, there is no group capable of challenging KFOR's control of the area. However, there is still violence in the territory. Because of a delay in deploying adequate numbers of international police, many reprisals have been taken against the Serbs and other minorities who have remained in Kosovo. This situation has prompted charges of ethnic cleansing in reverse, and about half of the prewar Serb population has fled the region since the end of the air war. Much of KFOR's mission has reverted to "policing" in order to stop the reprisals against the Serbs and others groups, but KFOR lacks sufficient numbers to meet the need.

Have the Combatants Been Disarmed and Demobilized?

As part of the agreement to end the air war, Serb forces were withdrawn from the province and the KLA agreed to an immediate cease-fire, disengaged from the zones of conflict, renounced the use of force, and demilitarized according to a timetable set out in the agreement signed between NATO and the KLA (UCK) on June 20, 1999. While the demilitarization largely has been carried out, the KLA was by no means a cohesive, unitary organization capable of commanding total authority over many that fought under its banner (Judah 2000). Several rival leaders within the organization claimed political authority in the aftermath of the air war, based on the role the KLA had played in fighting Serb forces on the ground.

The Kosovo Protection Corps (KPC) has been created to serve as a (theoretically) multiethnic civil emergency service agency under UNMIK authority and has made no secret of its desire to form the basis for a national army if Kosovo becomes independent. However, this force is regarded with some suspicion in the international community as several members have been suspected of organized crime, violent acts against minorities, illegal policing, and breaches of political neutrality (ICG 2002b).

On a practical level, the KPC provides employment for many former KLA fighters, largely keeping them from using their military skills in a manner that would undermine the stability of the current or future government. Although the KPC was initially established at a force level of five-thousand members, the intention was to gradually decommission about two-thousand of those into a reserve component. However, this process has been repeatedly delayed (ICG 2002b). At the same time, many elements associated with the former KLA remain strong in many parts of Kosovo and probably could re-form within a short period of time (Sell 2001).

Have the Basic Structures of the Rule of Law Been (Re)established?

In an exit interview before leaving his post as the head of UNMIK in January 2001, Dr. Bernard Kouchner said the biggest failure of international efforts in Kosovo has been "our inability to stop the violence, to offer enough protection to all the members of the community, the Serbs, and the other minorities" (Erlanger 2001). The UN special envoy for humanitarian affairs, Dennis McNamara, said that there had been an environment of "tolerance for intolerance" and revenge from the start. According to McNamara, a New Zealander, "there was no real effort or interest in trying to deter or stop it. There was an implicit endorsement of it by everybody—by the silence of the Albanian political leadership and by the lack of active discouragement of it by the West" (Erlanger 2000). Although retributions by Kosovar Albanians against Serbs and other minorities have declined over time, they remain frequent, and have prompted many Serbs to move into the northern area where they constitute a majority or seek refuge in Serbia.

Although several top Western leaders including President Clinton, Secretary of State Albright, and NATO Secretary-General Lord Robertson made statements warning the Albanians that the West could not continue its support for Kosovo if violence against minorities continued at such a pace and in such an organized fashion, little was done on the ground to prevent such attacks from occurring. Although the United Nations authorized a police force of around six thousand, only a third of that number had deployed by March 2000, ten months after external actors took over management of the province (*Economist* 2000a). While difficulties in obtaining police were in part due to the UN call for officers in East Timor at roughly the same time, many countries that had promised forces did not meet their commitments. In addition, many of the police volunteered by their governments were useless because they could not speak English or a local language, were not adequately trained in policing, or could not drive (*Economist* 2000a; Erlanger 2000). In early 2002, the force stood at approximately 4,400, slightly more than two-thirds of the authorized level (United Nations 2002).

Prior to 1999, UN police had only been authorized to train and mentor local police. Due in part to the lessons learned as a result of the experiences of the International Police Task Force (IPTF) in Bosnia, the United Nations gave its police forces in Kosovo and East Timor the authority to

arrest people and establish law and order. However, the international police force in Kosovo has been understaffed and outgunned—most are
armed with handguns, while many gangs they confront wield automatic
weapons. In the absence of an adequate police force, KFOR was forced to
commit about half of its manpower to protecting minorities and is providing a security presence in Serb areas (NATO 1999; White House 1999).

A local Kosovar force is being trained in a newly developed multiethnic
police academy run by the Organization for Security and Cooperation in
Europe (OSCE). This academy has graduated almost 4,400 officers by the
end of 2001, of whom 15 percent are minority and 18 percent women.
About 1,400 new candidates are expected to be trained in 2002 (ICG
2002b; United Nations 2002). However, because many of the recruits were
hastily chosen and trained, further background checks and monitoring are
needed before they are able to assume a greater role in public security. The
targeted overall strength of the Kosovo Police Service is 10,000 (United
Nations 2002).

When the international community stepped in after the air war in 1999,
Kosovo's legal system was in shambles. Much of the province's local judiciary had not been allowed to practice since 1989, so finding qualified people
as well as accessing the resources, equipment, and facilities were a challenge.
While the United Nations has struggled to set up an impartial judiciary, Serb
judges have faced intimidation and threats, and Albanian judges have found
it hard to convict a kinsman for attacking a Serb. Additionally, the meager
judicial salary of about two hundred dollars a month was not sufficient to
insulate judges from bribery (*Economist* 2000a). Witnesses have been intimidated or killed; of those actually arrested, many have been quickly released,
either because of the lack of prison space or the lack of resources to bring
them to trial (*Economist* 2000a; Erlanger 2000). Although there were about
five hundred killings in the first year of international control over the
province—a disproportionate number of them committed against Serbs and
other minorities—there was not a single conviction of anyone responsible
for any of the killings.

To combat these problems, UNMIK has pulled in international judges,
prosecutors, and defense lawyers to try cases as well as train their local
counterparts. It also has asked legal experts from the Council of Europe to
review the four major bodies of law that exist in Kosovo—the criminal code,
the criminal procedure code, the law on international peace and security,
and the penal law of Serbia—to create a coherent legal framework and to
make sure they are in conformity with internationally recognized human
rights standards.

To show its commitment to police and justice issues, UNMIK reestablished a Pillar I in May 2001 focused on these issues as part of its formal operational framework, and placing it under the direct responsibility of the
United Nations. (The original Pillar I focused on humanitarian assistance

and was phased out in June 2000.) However, although much progress has been made in securing the rule of law since 1999, many problems still remain. With no Constitutional Court to provide guidance (and little case law to serve as precedent), there is still confusion over applicable law. While international jurists and prosecutors are assigned to address potentially charged ethnic cases, bias continues to be a major issue, especially in the lower courts where the international presence is limited or nonexistent. Additionally, there is a shortage of prison space and a lack of a trained staff to run the prisons. UNMIK is working to establish the legal and structural framework for a system of parole, but, as of early 2002, the program had not been funded (ICG 2002b).

In addition to the concerns of personal safety and accountability, a new worry has arisen requiring competent policing and a functioning judiciary: organized crime. With the depressed economy and the lack of a legal system, there are growing concerns about crime syndicates (from Albania, in particular) expanding their activities into the region. The trade of heroin and trafficking of women have been cited, but concerns about the criminal penetration of politics, the evolution of the region into a Mafia republic, and links to terrorism have also been voiced (*Economist* 2000a; ICG 2002b; UNAUSA 2000; United Nations 2002). UNMIK is setting up five new specialized units to deal with the issue.

Have Refugees Been Repatriated and Internally Displaced People Returned to Their Homes?

As was discussed in relation to the evaluation of external actors in diffusing the short-term humanitarian crisis, great strides were made within a short period to return the large number of refugees and displaced persons to their homes. Although nearly one-third of the housing stock was destroyed and much of the rest subject to varying degrees of damage, most ethnic Albanian refugees that fled during the air war returned within a year of its conclusion.

However, the security situation for returns by the Kosovar Serbs has been a cause for concern. UNHCR has balked at supporting plans to return Serbs to the province, citing danger to their personal security. In February 2001, a bomb attack on a bus full of Serbs killed ten and injured dozens more, despite the presence of peacekeeping troops. Police officials say there is no doubt that the attack was intended to deter Serbs from returning at a time when they were winning international support after the ouster of Milošević (Gall 2001). To compound the concerns of the minority Serb community, three suspects arrested for the bombing were released in late 2001 because the intelligence information upon which their detention was based was ruled inadmissible in court. Under the criminal code in Kosovo, evidence gathered covertly may not be used as evidence in court.

Fewer than two thousand five hundred of the one hundred fifty to two hundred thousand Serbs who once lived in Kosovo have returned, and the first organized returns that began in the summer of 2001 have met with a variety of problems. For example, the eighty Serbs who returned in August with NATO escorts to the village of Zvecan have returned largely because they have nowhere else to go. Housed in tents and with no electricity at night, they are frustrated that home construction has proceeded far more slowly than anticipated. Part of the problem has been that the original plan was for the residents to rebuild their homes with donated materials, but most of the returnees are elderly and unable to do the construction (Henne- berger 2001). To recruit younger people to return, however, requires the availability of jobs, which are nonexistent in this largely destroyed Serbian village.

Have Political Authority and Institutions Been (Re)established in a Manner That Allows the Citizens of the Country to Hold Them Accountable for Their Actions?

If the high representative in Bosnia can be compared to the pope (in that he holds most of his power by virtue of moral authority), the SRSG (special representative of the secretary-general) heading the UN mission in Kosovo could be compared to a czar (or, according to Kitfield 2000, an imperial pasha). Having learned from past experiences in Somalia and Bosnia, the SRSG sits at the top of an international pyramid and has broad powers— such as the ability to enact laws—to implement the UN mandate. However, while this may solve some of the past problems of international administra- tion of societies in or coming out of conflict, several difficulties still remain. The Kosovo mission has been slowed by the cumbersome bureaucratic structure of the United Nations, the lack of unified support from members of the UN Security Council, and because KFOR still reports to NATO for operational purposes. Additionally, economic commitments from UN mem- ber states have been slow in coming and UNMIK's near insolvency has un- dermined its administrators' leverage in dealing with local parties (Rohde 2000; UNAUSA 2000).

To include Kosovars in the interim government, UNMIK set up a Joint Interim Administrative Structure (JIAS) in December 1999 as a means of sharing the responsibility for central and municipal administrative services. While the SRSG remained the head of the organization, he was advised by a thirty-six-member Kosovo Transitional Council (KTC), composed of se- lected members from Kosovo's political, religious, ethnic, and civic commu- nities. An Interim Advisory Council (IAC) served as an advisory cabinet to the SRSG and proposed policy guidelines for the twenty administrative de- partments, each co-chaired by a Kosovar and international staff representa- tive. The co-chair positions were shared by the three main Albanian political parties, three national communities (Serb, Bosnian, and Turk), and an independent. After the November 2001 elections, the twenty departments were consolidated into nine transitional departments, which then became formal ministries upon the establishment of the government.

At the local level, thirty municipal assemblies were elected to a two-year term in October 2000. These, in compliance with UNMIK regulations, appointed chief executive officers and members of their municipal boards. The boards act as the executive bodies at the local level and are responsible for the day-to-day running of services (United Nations 2001a). UNMIK administrators are progressively handing over management responsibilities to local authorities, with a view of fully disengaging in the future (United Nations 2002). The next round of municipal elections is set for September 2002.

In attempting to develop structures for self-government, UNMIK was hobbled by infighting among Albanians, especially by former members of the KLA (Judah 2000). In the absence of early elections to determine Kosovar leadership, numerous claimants presented themselves as speaking on behalf of the Kosovar people. While external actors have sought to avoid head-on collisions with Albanian leaders (which they see as a no-win situation), it has been difficult to know who had the legitimacy to speak on behalf of whom.

Although municipal elections were held in October 2000, many in the international community had sought to hold off on province-wide elections, arguing that they might legitimize hard-liners as they did in Bosnia, and also because they feared that a general election could be seen as the first step to Kosovar independence. Others—notably former SRSG Kouchner and Dayton negotiator and former U.S. Ambassador to the United Nations Richard Holbrooke—had argued that elections must be held quickly or frustrations would likely explode (Erlanger 2001; Holbrooke 2001). Additionally, many Kosovars feared that the international community's embrace of the new Yugoslav government and the arrest of Milošević might increase Western acceptance of Serbia's continued sovereignty over the province. Some suggested that too much delay in calling elections would result in Kosovars taking matters into their own hands, perhaps setting up a parallel state as they did in the early 1990s (Sell 2001).

In May 2001, SRSG Haekkerup promulgated a constitutional framework for Kosovo, overruled objections from both Albanians and Serbs, and set elections for that November. The framework laid out the legal basis for a system of self-government, including a 120-seat assembly. The assembly, which reserved ten seats for Serbs and ten more for Kosovo's other minorities, elects a president who, in turn, nominates a prime minister who will form a government. Under the framework, Kosovo will have wide-ranging autonomy for domestic matters, but external matters will remain under international control. The framework does not state when or how final status will be resolved, and it denied Albanian requests for a referendum on independence.

As was expected, Ibrahim Rugova's Democratic League of Kosovo (LDK) party won the largest share of the votes in the November election, taking about 46 percent of the total cast. Former KLA Commander Hashim Thaci's Democratic Party of Kosovo (PDK) received about 26 percent, and another ethnic-Albanian party, the Alliance for the Future of Kosovo (AAK) tallied just under 10 percent. Although many had feared the Serbs would not participate in the elections, after officials in Belgrade publicly called on them to do so, 46 percent turned out for the elections, garnering 11 percent of the total vote. The Serbs will end up with twenty-one seats in the assembly. Because of the constitutional framework requirement that at least 61 percent of the assembly vote in favor of a candidate for president, a three-month deadlock ensued after the election until the three leading Albanian parties were able to reach a compromise in late February 2002. The ultimate agreement, facilitated by the newly arrived SRSG Michael Steiner, paved the way for Rugova to become the first president and the PDK's senior lawmaker, Bajram Rexhepi, to become prime minister. One seat in the cabinet is reserved for a politician from the Serb community in Kosovo and another for a member of Kosovo's other minorities.

Is Economic Development Underway?

Until the political future of Kosovo is decided, economic reconstruction is, in many ways, paralyzed. Few private investors are willing to commit large sums of money while uncertain of the economic orientation of the province's future rulers. While Serbia may have theoretically embraced a free-market economy, in practice, many of the old attitudes and structures remain, and gains made in the province are easily reversible. Additionally, the inadequacy of the criminal justice and legal systems within Kosovo also deters private investment, leaving the area deeply dependent on international aid (USIP 2000a).

The Stability Pact for South Eastern Europe, signed in July 1999, commits Europe to promoting economic development in the region with the hope that it will encourage the needed reforms and foster the economic development necessary to join an integrated Europe. During 1999 and 2000, Europe provided more than $3 billion for civilian programs in Kosovo and the United States has given $900 million (Daalder and O'Hanlon 2000). However, with the basic infrastructure left over from Yugoslav communism already outdated before largely being destroyed in the war, major work needs to be done. Even before the damage from the air war, Kosovo was one of the poorest regions in Eastern—let alone all of—Europe. Compounding the difficulties in economic recovery, most of the southeastern European region is in the midst of a transition from a command to a free-market economy, with many countries suffering from balance-of-payments shocks, high unemployment, and inefficient production. Thus, the natural export markets for many of Kosovo's goods are suffering themselves. In an effort to enforce budget discipline, promote a banking industry, and reassure private investors, Kosovo adopted the euro as its main currency at the beginning of 2002. Additionally, UNMIK has worked with the Department of Trade and Industry to develop and promulgate assorted business regulations necessary for a market economy.

However, many problems remain. The province continues to suffer from severe power shortages, as Kosovo's two electrical plants do not function reliably, requiring much power to be imported from abroad. Other basic services such as running water, sewage, and telephones also are not consistently available (*Economist* 2000a; United Nations 2002). Additionally, after Milošević's retraction of autonomy in 1989, Belgrade transferred many Albanian-owned local enterprises to Serbs, leaving ownership muddled. Kosovo's current legal system remains unable to sort it out. Ownership issues and the need to establish a fair and transparent process are holding up privatization of the province's large conglomerates, leaving small businesses in the services and trading sectors to lead the recovery (Kohler 2000). However, in the absence of an orderly banking system, much of the economy has functioned on the barter system.

Has a Mechanism Been Developed to Deal with Past Atrocities and Promote Reconciliation between Groups?

Although the International Criminal Court for the former Yugoslavia (ICTY) indicted Yugoslav President Milošević (and four others) during the air war in 1999 for crimes against humanity and other transgressions resulting from his policies in Kosovo, it was not until eight months after he had been forced from power in October 2000 that Serbia—to the surprise of many inside and outside of Yugoslavia—turned Milošević over to the tribunal. His trial began in February 2002 and is expected to last at least two years.

However, many Albanian victims of atrocities committed by Serbian forces have yet to see action on their claims. Prosecutors at the ICTY have conceded that they cannot handle all of the cases. A Kosovo war crimes court was proposed by a commission of Albanian and international legal experts in 1999, but the idea languished as UNMIK tried to establish a local judiciary to deal with cases. However, in June 2000, SRSG Kouchner called for the creation of the Kosovo War and Ethnic Crimes Court (KWECC), recognizing that attempts to give the local judiciary a chance had failed (Gall 2000). The court was to be headed by international judges and prosecutors and supplemented by equal numbers of Albanian, Serbian, and other ethnic judges. It would try people accused of war crimes, crimes against humanity, genocide, and other serious crimes committed on the grounds of race, ethnicity, religion, nationality, association with an ethnic minority, or political opinion (USIP 2000b). However, there has been little movement to establish such a court, and Kouchner's successors have by-and-large sought to deal with the issues within the developing domestic court system.

Have Efforts Been Made to (Re)establish Local Governance, Encourage the Development of Civil Society, and Promote Community-Building Activities in General?

With Kosovo subject to the ethnic cleansing of Albanians by the Serbs in 1998 and early 1999—and then of Serbs by Albanians in the aftermath of the air war—ethnic tensions remain very high, and the appetite for revenge continues to undermine the prospects for peace (Judah 2000).

The media also has inflamed nationalist tensions and tested the limits of free speech in the province. The Albanian newspaper *Bota Sot* has described Serbs as barbarous, brutal, and blood sucking, claimed that Serbian children are born killers (and as such will remain for all their lives) and that they are trained to plant land mines. The paper has also stated that all Serbs "who are living today in Kosovo are criminals," that "revenge is a natural instinct," and asserted that NATO peacekeepers have staged attacks on Serbs so that blame will be directed at innocent ethnic Albanians (Smith 2000). Although UNMIK promulgated a new regulation banning the spread of "hatred, discord, and intolerance" whenever it seems likely to disturb public order, the organization has been reluctant to act against the newspaper, fearing to do so would smack of censorship and that its actions would be compared with Milošević's closure of independent media outlets in Yugoslavia.

The Serbs, on the other hand, largely view themselves as the victims and are inclined to take the position that the history of human rights abuses in Kosovo began with the Albanian campaign against them after the 1999 war. They tend to ignore the role many Kosovar Serbs played in the ten-year repression of the Albanians in the 1990s and the well-documented attacks against, and uprooting of, Albanian civilians in 1998 and 1999 (Sell 2001).

The thirty municipal assemblies elected in October 2000 have largely assumed responsibilities for the day-to-day running of services in their areas, albeit under international supervision. UNMIK has also tried to implement a series of confidence-building measures focusing on multiethnic initiatives, the creation of communal marketplaces, and targeted economic development (United Nations 2001b). In addition to the formal governing structures, USAID's Office of Transition Initiatives (OTI) has designed a number of programs to aid local communities, indigenous media organizations, and

NGOs. Bringing together a mixture of local authorities, community groups, NGO members, local technical experts, and interested citizens into what it calls Community Improvement Councils (CICs), OTI has sought to identify and prioritize community projects to which it provides funding. Projects have included restoring and improving public services (e.g., roads, water, electricity, sanitation); reconstructing and repairing homes, schools, health clinics, and community centers; setting up media programs to ensure that fair and objective information is available to all Kosovars; and providing supplies and spare parts for agricultural equipment (OTI 2000a). By November 2000, OTI had funded more than 250 small-scale community improvement projects and had established in excess of 220 CICs around Kosovo. OTI (2000a) claims that the experience of working together in a participatory, democratic, and constructive manner is as important as the humanitarian impact of the projects themselves.

Do Citizens Support Belonging to the Political Entity?

Almost all of the ethnic Albanians in Kosovo wish to become independent, while almost all of the ethnic Serbs in the province wish to remain a part of Serbia. However, the overwhelming opinion of the rest of the region, with the exception of Albania and the Albanian parts of Macedonia, is that independence would be dangerous and destabilizing. President Boris Trajkovski of Macedonia argues that the region cannot survive if the international community allows groups to redraw borders and boundaries, making smaller units of even purer ethnic states (Bildt 2001).

SUMMARY AND CONCLUSIONS

In 1989, at a ceremony commemorating the 600th anniversary of the Battle of Kosovo, President Milošević revoked Kosovo's autonomous status. While early protests were confined to peaceful means, ethnic Albanians in Kosovo viewed the European Union's decision to recognize the Federal Republic of Yugoslavia (after the Dayton Peace Accords were signed in 1995 ending the Bosnian conflict) as removing the international leverage that could force Milošević to respect their rights in the province. After the KLA initiated an armed revolt in 1997 and Milošević responded with increasing levels of brutality, NATO eventually undertook a seventy-eight-day bombing campaign in 1999, forcing Serbian troops from the province.

Once a decision to act was made, external efforts to manage Kosovo took advantage of many—but by no means all—of the lessons from efforts in Bosnia. In the reconstruction effort after the air war, reasonably well thought out plans were put in place. However, Kosovo was not simply a repeat of Bosnia, and many activities did not always flow according to the plan. Additionally, many of the bureaucratic problems with the United

Nations and many of the domestic difficulties of NATO members securing legislative approval for aid commitments that had dogged the previous efforts still played a role.

For better or worse, the success of the external efforts to bring peace and stability to Kosovo likely will temper future decisions to undertake such ambitious mandates. If it succeeds, it may set a precedent that the international community can—and perhaps should—become involved in at least some of the many violent internal conflicts around the world. On the other hand, if it fails or even ends up inconclusive, requiring international forces to be committed indefinitely, the United Nations, NATO, and especially the United States likely will back away from future missions of this sort. If the international community could not deal with the small European province of Kosovo given the high levels of military and economic resources committed to it, the argument goes, it will not be successful elsewhere.

No one can be satisfied with the current situation in Kosovo. Between 1998 and mid-1999, more than ten thousand people were killed and nearly a million people were pushed from their homes. Although the eleven-week bombing campaign in 1999 ended the ethnic cleansing of Albanians by the Serbs and pushed Serb forces out of the province, the Kosovar Albanians subsequently returned and, in turn, forced almost three quarters of the two hundred thousand Serbs who had lived in the province before war to flee.

While the jury is still out on the success or failure of the overall mission, certain interim assessments can be made, especially with regard to the state-building foundations addressed in this paper. The first and most glaring issue is the lack of resolution of the province's future political status. The overwhelming majority of the Kosovar population insists upon independence, which is exactly what many members of the international community—both inside and outside of the Balkan Region—fear would lead to greater regional destabilization. While the issue will not be easy to resolve, a path must be chosen, as much of the institutional and economic development is in a holding pattern until then.

Although there are occasional clashes with organized, armed groups and discoveries of caches of weapons hidden in the countryside, the KLA has been disbanded and KFOR is in control of the territory. However, there is no local force capable of taking over that role in the near term, and it is not likely that one can be developed that could withstand the armies of regional states if Kosovo were to become an independent state.

The inability to deploy sufficient numbers of well-trained international civilian police officers in the wake of the air war was perhaps the international community's most glaring—and preventable—failure. The failure to deter reprisals against Serbs and other minorities forced external actors to fight an uphill battle to restore public order. The lack of policing and of accountability in the absence of a judicial system has meant that Albanians could undertake reprisals without fear of consequences. Although the court system is slowly being developed—largely staffed by international jurists—true "rule of law" is a long way off for the residents of Kosovo.

In terms of establishing institutions capable of promoting a resolution of the roots of the conflict, some progress has been made, especially at the local level. Hopes have also been raised that the province-wide elections held in November 2001 will devolve greater levels of responsibility to the Kosovars themselves and lead to more permanent institutions of government. However, in the absence of an agreement on the final status of the province, all institutional development will be provisional. Economic development of the region has occurred to some extent, but, because of the legacy of communism and the need to create the foundations of a market economy, progress has been slow. Additionally, in the absence of a final settlement and the rule of law, private investment has been limited.

While local elections have been held and many community development activities are taking place, most do not span the divide between the Albanian and Serb communities. Ethnic divisions still dominate all forms of activity and little headway has been made in promoting reconciliation between the groups.

The conflict in Kosovo is in many ways an extension of the wars of the early 1990s in Croatia and Bosnia, as different groups in the former Yugoslavia struggle to define their nationhood and place in the international system today. Unfortunately, the air war did not end the struggle between the Kosovar Albanians and Serbs, and also may have had the unfortunate side effect of kindling a number of fires between the minority Albanian populations and the dominant Slavic groups in several surrounding states. Until the issue of ethnicity and nationhood is resolved in a manner acceptable to all of the peoples in the region, there will not be self-sustaining peace—with or without a NATO presence.

NOTES

1. While many local sources refer to the region as Kosova, this chapter will refer to the region as Kosovo as is common in most U.S. publications.

2. The common refrain heard today that "Kosovo is to the Serbs what Jerusalem is to the Jews" appeared about the same time (if not slightly later). The Patriarchate, after being defunct for 154 years, was re-created in 1920.

3. The KLA also is often referred to as the UCK, which is the Albanian-language acronym.

4. The G-8 is comprised of the seven leading industrial states plus Russia. The principles are included as Annex 1 to UN Security Council Resolution 1244 adopted June 10, 1999.

CHAPTER 6

DRAWING LESSONS FROM PAST EXPERIENCES

While conflict may be inevitable, the levels of violence reached in Somalia, Bosnia, and Kosovo were not. While primary responsibility for the atrocities committed falls on the domestic actors in those countries, the international community was well aware of each country's slide toward that end and took little concerted action to avert it. Only after large-scale humanitarian crises were well under way did external actors take firm action to alleviate the suffering and attempt to end the violence.

However, once external actors did decide to act, they realized that stopping the violence was only a part of what was needed to create a stable peace. External actors then undertook a mission that has been variously termed "nationbuilding," "statebuilding," or "peacebuilding" in an attempt to prevent a return to violence. Although the United States and other Western democracies have assisted other countries as they have attempted to move from authoritarian—or even communist—systems to a democracy, the scale of efforts in this study's three countries were of much greater magnitude.

As we have learned from the experiences of several southern European countries in the 1970s and many Latin American regimes in the 1980s and 1990s, there is great uncertainty in the transition from an authoritarian regime to "something else" and that this transition is by no means a linear or rational process (O'Donnell and Schmitter 1986). Somalia, Bosnia, and Kosovo have reinforced these lessons and, when one adds the ethnopolitical dimension evident in each of these struggles (largely absent in previous transitions), it is readily apparent that there is no simple solution—no magic bullet—to resolve these complex and deeply rooted conflicts (Gurr 1996).

It is in this context that I have sought to examine what external actors have done in their efforts to bring peace to these countries and to evaluate how well they have laid the foundation for (re)constructing a capable, effective, and legitimate state in each. In a general sense, one can argue that international action in each of these countries has left it in a better position than it was previously and, in that broad sense, should be viewed as achieving a level of success. The creation of a longer-term foundation, however, has proven elusive.

In general terms, many of the issues included in my list of questions assessing statebuilding outlined in chapter 2 and explored in the case studies were at least recognized and addressed at some level (along with numerous other issues beyond my scope). However, while many important activities were carried out, I do not believe sufficient focus was placed upon those factors identified as necessary to create a capable, effective, and legitimate state.

So, what did we learn from these efforts? While one cannot arrive at conclusive answers from three case studies, lessons can be drawn from them that are likely to be applicable in future statebuilding efforts. In all, I have drawn twenty-three lessons from the case studies. The first nine are general lessons that are broadly applicable to external interventions and set the framework within which statebuilding takes place. The second set of fourteen lessons applies specifically to the statebuilding efforts in the country. In each case, they are listed as much as possible in the order in which they apply, and it should not be construed that the later lessons are less important than the earlier ones.

GENERAL LESSONS

Lesson 1: Internal actors often are unable to stop the violence and bring about a resolution of the conflict, especially if the forces inciting the conflict have an external benefactor.

In each of the cases in this study, the internal groups that sought to bring about a resolution of the conflict were unable to counter the powerful forces with weapons that had an interest in continuing the conflict. The leaders of these forces generally sought to secure political or financial gains that would be unavailable to them in a peaceful, democratic society. While this is not necessarily a new phenomenon, the forced starvation and scale of atrocities perpetrated against civilians—often simply because of their ethnicity—is. External actors have realized that, in the absence of their actions, great suffering would continue to occur.

In Somalia, the traditional mediating institution of the clan elders was rendered largely ineffective by armed militias who were reaping great profits and enhanced political status in the context of the violence. There was little incentive for those with this new wealth and power to relinquish their gains and return to their previous semi-subsistence life. In Bosnia, nationalist Serb leaders knew their political powers would be greatly circumscribed in a new Bosnian state in which they would be a minority. Hence, they sought to secure as much land as they could by militarily dominating it and, in the process, cleansing it of all non-Serbs. In this effort, they had a ready supply of weapons available from their ethnic brethren in neighboring Serbia. In the aftermath of the Dayton Accords, many of these nationalist leaders still retain levels of influence and continue to resist changes in the political and economic realms that would undermine their authority or subject them to prosecution. In Kosovo, ethnic Albanians simply were unable to counter the well-equipped Serb military forces dispatched from Belgrade.

Lesson 2: Early action may save lives, create a more positive environment for peace, and require less international assistance.

Many recent studies have touted the benefits of preventative action (Cortright 1997; Jentleson 2000; Snow 2000; Woodward 2000). While it is easy to state that preventing the slide into anarchy and mass deaths is obviously preferable, it is difficult to secure the international support and mobilize the resources to do so, especially when other more significant concerns are clouding the horizon. However, once passions are inflamed and atrocities committed, it is much more difficult to bring about peace and reconciliation. Special Representative of the UN Secretary-General (SRSG) Sahnoun (1994, xiii) asserted, "if the international community had intervened earlier and more effectively in Somalia, much of the catastrophe that has unfolded could have been avoided." One can argue that prevention should have been taken well before the civil war broke out in 1988, and that U.S. (as well as Italian and some British) military assistance undoubtedly kept Siad Barre in power longer than he would have remained otherwise. While this may have been justified in terms of cold war interests, this external support likely contributed to the onset and severity of the civil war.

The conflicts in Bosnia and Kosovo were each a consequence of the disintegration of Yugoslavia and each displayed numerous warning signs of impending large-scale conflict. In the aftermath of Croatia's secession from the Federal Republic of Yugoslavia (FRY), it was clear that Bosnia would soon follow suit and that Serb forces would resist it. In Kosovo, the downward spiral started after Milošević rescinded the province's autonomy in 1989 and began in earnest after the formation of the Kosovo Liberation Army (KLA) in 1997 and Milošević's brutal response to it. However, earlier action in the Balkans would have forced the international community to develop a consensus on the difficult issues of the rights of secession and muscular peacekeeping when the West was largely hoping to prevent the disintegration of the Soviet Union and avoid further military action in the wake of the Persian Gulf War and the deaths of the U.S. Army Rangers in Somalia.

Lesson 3: There is no such thing as a purely humanitarian operation in the midst of internal conflict.

External actors avoided the establishment of a political agenda for early actions in Somalia, seeking only to provide humanitarian assistance to starving people. It was not until UNOSOM II was formed that a mandate was undertaken to deal with the collapsed state. With the benefit of hindsight, it was naïve and unrealistic to think that the international community's provision of food and role as a mediator would be able to remedy Somalia's vast problems or that the political, military, and humanitarian aspects of intervention could be separated (Crocker 1995; Hirsch and Oakley 1995). Starvation in Somalia was used as both a weapon to displace persons from their land and as an instrument of leverage to secure resources from the international community. In this sense, providing refugees and displaced persons with food had political as well as humanitarian implications. In many respects, the lack of a combined political, military, and humanitarian operation increased the power of the warlords who had little interest in a return to stability and who sought to undermine the moderate and unarmed elements in society.

External actors attempted to respond to the early phases of the Bosnian crisis largely by sending UN peacekeepers charged with providing humanitarian aid. However, the main problem in Bosnia was not a humanitarian crisis that could be alleviated by the delivery of food and medicine, but was an attempt by a minority group to dominate an area largely occupied by people from another ethnic group. Because the Serb goal was to cleanse the area of non-Serb peoples, they attempted to thwart efforts to provide sustenance to those they sought to remove. In Kosovo, it would have been unrealistic to expect the international community to provide for the needs of the hundreds of thousands of ethnic Albanians displaced by Milošević's actions (even before the air war) without attempting to deal with the cause of their displacement.

Lesson 4: In order for a statebuilding mission to be successful, external actors must be in general agreement on the goals—and largely on the means used to secure those goals. They also must agree to act in concert and be committed for the long term.

Unless external actors develop a joint strategy, internal actors often are able to deflect and diffuse any pressure to change behavior. While developing a joint strategy is difficult to do—especially in the early phases of a conflict—limited, uncoordinated actions may be counterproductive, encouraging internal actors to rebel. By demonstrating that the costs of action would be high and likely would not be successful, the internal actors may attempt to undermine domestic support for the action in the external actors' home states.

In Somalia, there was general agreement on resolving the humanitarian crisis and preventing the starvation of hundreds of thousands of people.

However, once that objective was largely met, there was far less consensus on the UN mission. While UNOSOM II was given a far-reaching mandate, it was not given the support and resources to carry it out, encouraging local resistance by those who saw the goals of the mission as threatening their power. There was also little consensus that the hunt for Aideed was the best way to deal with Somalia's problems, as quickly became apparent when the United States and many European powers announced the withdrawal of their troops after the deaths of the U.S. Army Rangers.

In Bosnia, Serb forces were able to act with relative impunity and to disregard UN actions from 1993 to mid-1995, until the United States and the Europeans were able to reach an agreement on a course of action. However, when an acceptable framework for peace was developed, NATO was able to take resolute action that, in concert with the expulsion of Serbs from the Krajina Region by Croatian armed forces and Milošević's willingness to back away from support for the Bosnian Serbs, was able to bring the parties to the bargaining table.

In Kosovo, a number of cleavages within the international community were at work. First, while the United States and Western Europe deplored Milošević's actions against the Kosovar Albanians, they disagreed on the requisites for effective action. The United States supported air strikes and refused to consider putting U.S. troops on the ground. The Europeans, on the other hand, feared a repeat of the ineffective air strikes in Bosnia in early 1995, and argued that air strikes must be backed by the threat of ground action if they were to be effective. Second, Russia, recouping its ability to act internationally, let it be known that it did not favor international military action against its Slavic brethren, the Serbs. Milošević counted on this support to blunt action against him.

Third, while regretting the actions of Milošević, many countries feared that the notion of sovereign control of a state would be eroded by the precedent of the international community taking action against a government on behalf of a minority. With minorities seeking to secede in Russia (Chechnya), China (Tibet), India (Kashmir), and a number of other countries, many feared the precedent would set off a chain of separatist fighting that would destabilize many countries (Snow 2000). And finally, many lesser-developed countries saw action in Kosovo as setting a double standard. They claimed it was hypocritical for the international community to take action against a European dictator who was forcefully displacing large numbers of people yet killing relatively few (by developing world standards), but not raise a finger to rid many African countries of brutal dictators who were displacing and slaughtering people by much greater numbers.

In view of these cleavages, there was little hope any action could be undertaken by the United Nations. Ultimately, the United States and Europe sought to force diplomatic action through the threat of air strikes, agreeing essentially to defer a decision on ground troops. When the Serbs rejected the

Rambouillet agreement, NATO undertook what it expected to be a reasonably short air offensive. Russia reacted by severing all ties with NATO, and NATO scrambled to apply even greater pressure on Milošević to concede. However, as the weeks passed and the bombing began to destroy the Yugoslav infrastructure affecting the citizens of Serbia proper, the United States, Europe, and Russia were finally able to agree to a set of principles upon which an agreement could be based, effectively leaving Milošević little choice but to consent.

Lesson 5: U.S.-led and NATO forces have been effective at halting the violence and imposing a peace for as long as they remain there in force. However, statebuilding requires effecting changes that the military is unable to bring about.

The U.S.-led Unified Task Force (UNITAF) mission in Somalia and NATO forces in Bosnia and Kosovo have been successful at quelling the violence and enforcing a period of peace. However, while this is a necessary condition for laying the foundation of a capable, effective, and legitimate state, it has proven that it is by no means a sufficient one. Military forces can be effective at achieving military goals. However, they have a limited impact in shaping political goals, and virtually have no ability to bring about economic development, ethnic reconciliation, and many of the other essential tasks in (re)constructing a state (Snow 2000).

Although UNITAF made it clear it was not interested in rebuilding the Somali state, NATO forces in Bosnia and Kosovo both were parts of larger missions that intended to bring long-term peace to the societies. However, while some have faulted the Implementation Force (IFOR) and the Stabilization Force (SFOR) in Bosnia for not doing more to arrest war criminals and enforce freedom of movement and minority returns, the military forces have kept a relative peace for more than five years, underscoring the point that halting the violence alone has not brought about the necessary changes in society to ensure that such a peace would remain in their absence.

Lesson 6: Unless a new commitment is found to develop the necessary means, UN forces should not be assigned to an area where fighting is likely. If military action is needed, it should be left to a capable national force or an organization such as NATO.

In the early stages of international intervention in Somalia and Bosnia, UN peacekeepers were dispatched under Chapter VI provisions. In these chaotic environments, the lightly armed peacekeepers found themselves outnumbered, outgunned, unable to carry out their missions, and, on several occasions, taken hostage. In Somalia, the ineffectiveness of the UN mission gave way to the U.S.-led UNITAF forces that promptly overwhelmed local forces, allowing relief supplies to reach their intended recipients. After completing their narrowly defined mission, UNITAF forces withdrew, handing security back to the United Nations, which granted its UNOSOM II forces Chapter VII authority. However, it was quickly apparent to Aideed's forces that the broader authority did not overcome the weaknesses of the UN peacekeepers, and the country slowly slid back into chaos.

In Bosnia, UN peacekeepers were initially deployed to open the Sarajevo airport and ensure the safe delivery of aid around the city. The mandate later was changed to a Chapter VII mission and charged with ensuring distribution of aid around the country. However, neither mission was capable of deterring Serbs bent on capturing and ethnically cleansing Bosnian territory. After several episodes of peacekeepers being taken hostage, the external actors pulled them back into areas under full UN control, abandoning designated "safe areas" to the Serbs, and undertook sustained NATO air strikes to punish Serb militias. With the credibility of the UN peacekeepers undermined, the Bosniacs and Croats insisted upon a NATO force to execute the terms of the Dayton Accords. Militia forces never seriously tested the well-organized and well-equipped NATO soldiers.

In Kosovo, NATO (rather than the United Nations) took the lead from the beginning, with the Western nations knowing that action under UN auspices would surely be precluded by Security Council vetoes from Russia and China. Although unarmed Organization for Security and Cooperation in Europe (OSCE) monitors had been deployed into the province after the October 1998 agreement, they were withdrawn before the air war in order to ensure that the hostage episodes of Bosnia were not repeated. In the negotiations to end the bombing, NATO insisted that it—not the United Nations—lead the security force that would handle the cease-fire, although it did allow for the participation of a Russian security force.

Lesson 7: Exit strategies for security forces must be predicated on the achievement of certain objectives, not externally mandated dates.

Although useful for budgetary considerations and securing domestic political support in the states of the external actors, exit strategies based on an arbitrary period of time rather than the achievement of certain objectives have a counterproductive effect on the mission's ability to make and/or consolidate gains (de Jounge Oudraat 1999; Sharp 1997). If domestic actors know that a military force will only be in place for a limited period of time, they will resist implementing unpopular measures (such as disarming and demobilizing) and bide their time until the clock runs out. In this vein, the U.S. force in Bosnia has been accused of being designed "to leave as soon as possible, with as few casualties as possible, rather than to do whatever was necessary, for as long as necessary, to keep (or make) the peace" (Mandelbaum 1996).

Lesson 8: The United Nations must undertake fundamental reforms if it is to play a significant role in future statebuilding operations.

While many of the problems in UN operations—such as matching a mandate with the means to carry it out—can be traced to the lack of clear, strong, and sustained support (financial and otherwise) from the member states, a number of problems can also be traced to the organizational management, bureaucratic structure, and institutional culture of the United Nations itself. In each of the operations, the United Nations has experienced major deficiencies in deploying, staffing, and managing activities in the field. Many of these shortcomings have been recognized and identified by the Report of the Panel on United Nations Peace Operations (the "Brahimi Report") provided to the UN secretary-general and the president of the UN Security Council in August 2000.

The United Nations took on thirteen new peacekeeping missions between 1989 and 1992, the same number as had been undertaken between 1945 and 1988. In 1989, there were eight thousand peacekeepers; in 1994, there were eighty thousand. The Somali operation with its broad mandate was the victim of an overstretched, understaffed, underfunded, inexperienced, and poorly organized UN peacekeeping staff (Hirsch and Oakley 1995).

Shortly after the establishment of the United Nations Operation in Somalia (UNOSOM) in 1992, the UN office responsible for peacekeeping operations was reorganized and renamed the Department of Peacekeeping Operations (DPKO). While the objective was to bring the political, operational, logistical, civil police, de-mining, training, personnel, and administrative aspects of peacekeeping operations under one umbrella, planning and coordination of operations still suffered, and budgetary fights among groups ended up undermining important aspects of the mission, such as policing. The special representatives of the UN secretary-general (SRSGs) also found themselves bounced between different UN departments, unable to secure the needed resources and commitments. Additionally, the frequent turnover of high-level UN personnel—both civilian and military—compounded the difficulties.

In Bosnia, the UN does not play the overarching role it did in Somalia or continues to play in Kosovo, but the tasks that it does manage, such as the International Police Task Force (IPTF), have suffered from lack of funds and equipment. In Kosovo, the UN Interim Administration Mission (UNMIK) has been continually hampered by a slow response to needs in the field. Only six professional staff members in the New York UN headquarters support the $410 million-a-year program (UNAUSA 2001).

Lesson 9: Conflicts are best resolved and economic development brought about in a regional context.

There are essentially two reasons to do so: first, to prevent a regional actor from continuing to destabilize the peace and, second, to bring about greater economic and social integration to stabilize the peace.

In the cases of Bosnia and Kosovo, the underlying problem was the same: Serbia was attempting to help local Serbs retain dominance in areas where they were a minority. If the international community had taken a more comprehensive and longer-term approach to the area in dealing with the breakup of Yugoslavia in the early 1990s, much—although certainly not all—of the bloodshed may have been averted. Several scholars have claimed that, if the international community had secured agreements on the protection of minority rights as a precondition for international recognition, the scale of violence likely would not have reached the levels that it did (Galtung and Mushakoji 1999; Hagen 1999). Although Yugoslav assistance to Serbs in Bosnia and Kosovo has been largely stopped, the longer-term stability in the Balkans still is greatly dependent upon actions taken by Belgrade.

Additionally, both Bosnia and Kosovo suffer from the economic malaise emanating from the centrally planned economic structures of the former Yugoslavia. Economic development is predicated on a renewal of regional trade and the eventual integration into European economic structures. Recognizing this, the EU has developed a regional strategy to deal with all of the southeastern European countries.

Although the regional context was less relevant in the case of Somalia than in the Balkans, it still played a role. A number of the militias were able to secure weapons and supplies from their clan brethren in neighboring states and the famine aggravating the civil conflict extended well beyond Somalia's borders.

STATEBUILDING LESSONS

Lesson 1: The international community needs to take a more "holistic" approach to state reconstruction. Military, economic, and social programs must be better coordinated in order to leverage reforms and create a solid structure.

Many argue that economic development is the key to long-term state reconstruction; people who can secure a decent standard of living have a vested interest in peace. However, as all three cases demonstrate, a country cannot undertake serious economic development in the absence of personal security and an overall political framework upon which there is general agreement. Security and political agreement, however, will not come until the people within the territory develop a sense of community so that they can designate an authority from among themselves to develop the institutions and laws necessary to regulate society. However, this sense of community often will not come until some level of economic development is achieved so that people lengthen their time horizons and work for a better future.

So it is in this "Catch-22" situation that the international community must build on all three dimensions at the same time. This is not to say that the international community cannot prioritize, but that it cannot neglect one of the three legs of the "stool." The external actors must plan their activities and use their resources in a concerted manner to secure achievements across the board. In Somalia, the military activities under UNITAF were not only almost totally separated from the institutional, economic, and social aspects of the operation, they were also divorced from many security-related tasks, including disarming and demobilizing fighters, reestablishing the basic structures of the rule of law, and even promoting an agreement to end the conflict. Although UNOSOM II had a broader mandate to deal with many of the functions across all three dimensions, it had insufficient resources and support to do so. It should be no wonder that the statebuilding effort in Somalia failed.

In Bosnia, while there is better communication, NATO still leads the military operation while a "high representative" selected by backers of the Dayton Accords runs the political, economic, and social aspects of the mission. Civilian authorities largely have been unable to use NATO to gain leverage over reintegration and economic development efforts. The two structures were—at least theoretically—coordinated in Kosovo by the special representative of the UN secretary-general, who would direct the entire international community efforts there. However, on a practical level, the Kosovo Force (KFOR) remains operationally under control of NATO. Additionally, the absence of a political settlement over the future status of the province has delayed long-term planning until that issue is resolved.

In addition to security concerns, the economic front has seen improvements but still lacks the coordination necessary to pressure needed reforms. In Somalia, almost all economic and community development work was handled on a bilateral basis. There was a little more coordination in Bosnia with the advent of donors' conferences, but (often for domestic political reasons) donors still tended to give money bilaterally. In Kosovo, there has been an effort to centralize and prioritize the distribution of aid and programming, but many countries are reluctant to put their money into a pot run by the United Nations, which, in many eyes, has turned bureaucratization and inefficiency into an art form.

Lesson 2: External actors should designate a single head to synchronize the military, political, economic, and humanitarian aspects of the mission.

This is an area where later missions "learned" from earlier efforts. In large part because of the experiences in Somalia and Bosnia, the head of the UN mission in Kosovo has much more formal authority than those of preceding missions, although, in practice, he still has many impediments to carrying out his responsibilities. Much of the difficulty grows from the need to be accountable to a sponsoring organization, but conflicts also have arisen from the different organizational cultures of the military groups, the United Nations and other intergovernmental organizations, national governmental organizations (such as USAID), and nongovernmental organizations (NGOs).

In Somalia, lack of coordination among efforts to mediate the conflict allowed the warring parties to play concessions secured in one negotiation off against those in another. Additionally, no clear relationship was established between the U.S.-led UNITAF and the ongoing UNOSOM I, and faction leaders and NGOs found themselves negotiating with both. This lack of coordination greatly undermined the ability of external actors to exert leverage over recalcitrant parties.

In Bosnia, NATO forces report directly to NATO headquarters, while civilian efforts are loosely linked through the Office of the High Representative. While the high representative's powers to coordinate efforts still are limited, they are much greater than those originally given to him in the aftermath of the Dayton Accords. However, issues such as enforcing freedom of movement, the rights of minorities to return, and arresting war criminals continue to be a source of contention between the two sides (Bair and Dziedzic 1998; Sharp 1997; Wentz 1998).

Lesson 3: There must be a comprehensive agreement to resolve the conflict (not just a cease-fire) that is generally acceptable to all major groups of society upon which the international community can seek to rebuild important structures of the state.

This, obviously, is easier said than done, especially if some groups still hope to achieve gains through continued fighting. Having said this, all peace agreements are not created equal, and it is very important to get the terms right from the start. It is extremely difficult to renegotiate the contentious issues later, and a bad agreement can institutionalize all sorts of destabilizing factors that undermine the long-term foundations of a stable peace.

While the basic issue resolved by a treaty is choosing who will rule in the aftermath of the conflict, the most successful treaties institutionalize security guarantees for the various groups in society, disperse power among different institutions and different segments of society, and introduce a means of enforcing accountability (Hartzell 1999; Lake and Rothchild 1998; Linz and Stepan 1996; Schedler 1999). A lasting solution to civil war also depends upon the creation of a peace that takes into account the desires and grievances that drove people to war in the first place and which recognizes that a return to the status quo ante may not be sufficient (Keen 2000). It is also important to recognize that the more dominant sectors (especially those who previously ruled without constraints) have the most to lose in the process and will likely be the most reluctant to agree to its terms. In some cases, it may be necessary to impose peace on a reluctant party, but in doing so, the international community must be cognizant that this will necessitate a well-equipped security force and likely involve a long-term operation.

While there is no one-size-fits-all peace plan and each agreement must be tailored to the specific parties and specific circumstances of the conflict, external actors have a number of assets with which they can influence negotiations. They can exert pressure on recalcitrant parties through threats of military actions or sanctions, they can provide incentives through economic and/or military assistance, and they can promise entrance into regional organs such as the European Union in reward for certain actions. External actors can also reduce security fears through the deployment of military forces and the design of institutional safeguards so that one group is not able to gain control of the coercive apparatus of the state and use it against another group.

As difficult as a good, comprehensive agreement is to achieve, Somalia and Kosovo demonstrate the ramifications of trying to (re)construct the state in the absence of one. In Somalia, although most of the large-scale efforts were directed at trying to bring about such an agreement, Aideed, the strongest of the factional leaders, had little reason to reach an agreement that did not give him ultimate power. While one can debate whether removing Aideed would have solved anything, or whether or not Somalia was a case in which peace needed to have been imposed, there was no international consensus on the best course of action, much less a commitment to see it through.

In Kosovo, a cease-fire ending the air war was brought about once Milošević agreed to the principles upon which a final settlement would be reached. However, the principles basically established a *process* to reach a final settlement, but included no timetable and left the process heavily dependent on the international community. Complicating the resolution of the final status is that, although there is general agreement by major international actors that the independence of the province may be destabilizing to the region, the overwhelming number of domestic actors insists upon exactly that. The international community recognizes that if independence is not given to the province, any other solution developed likely would have to be imposed upon an uncooperative Kosovar population. Because of this dichotomy, external actors are dragging their feet on the ultimate resolution of the future political status of the province, which is breeding growing resentment within the population. Meanwhile, efforts to develop the province institutionally, economically, and socially, and to encourage reconciliation with the Serb minority are largely paralyzed, awaiting the resolution of the political situation.

In Bosnia, a relatively comprehensive settlement was signed in 1995. However, one of the parties—the Bosnian Serbs—was not in attendance. As is typical in many treaties, negotiations must at times gloss over details with broad diplomatic brush strokes in order to facilitate an agreement by the warring parties. The Dayton Accords leave a number of issues open to interpretation and include several features that impede progress toward developing a capable, efficient, and legitimate state. The security agreement allows each ethnic group to retain its armed forces, leaving the country with three separate armies, greatly facilitating the ability of each to return to armed conflict. The entities retain most of the power, reinforcing the ethnic division of the country. Calls by some Bosnian Croats to divide the Muslim-Croat Federation threaten to further complicate matters. Additionally, the electoral process has been cumbersome and has reinforced nationalist elements.

Lesson 4: Policing must be provided and the establishment of an environment based on the rule of law must be enforced from the beginning.

Although military forces conduct most of the security functions during a conflict and in the immediate aftermath of a cease-fire or peace agreement, the importance of having adequate police forces to deal with small-scale violence in the follow-on phase largely fell through the cracks in each of these three case studies. On one level, there were organizational problems because policing is generally handled by a different organization than traditional military or even peacekeeping tasks. But, on another level, while public pronouncements often stressed the importance of the role of policing, few actions were taken to back up the words with the funds, personnel, and commitment necessary to see the task through.

Policing should be complementary to the peacekeeping tasks of the military forces. Once the military has stabilized the security environment, police units should be deployed in large numbers to enforce the rule of law and prevent reprisals and other small-scale violence. To this end, there have been a number of recent calls (including those by former UNMIK head Bernard Kouchner and his counterpart in East Timor, Sergio Vieria de Mello) to develop a trained reserve force of international police that could be deployed on short notice (Brahimi 2000; Plunkett 1998; UNAUSA 2000). The experiences of the countries in this study highlight the need for such a force. In most instances, it would deal with the small-scale violence in the population centers and that targeted against relief efforts, but it should also be capable of arresting war criminals (although military forces may need to supplement this effort for the worst offenders), managing riots, and helping restructure and train local police forces. The force could be trained in advance within its home country by UN advisors according to internationally determined standards and deployed in national units, working closely with military units in each sector.

In most ongoing conflicts (and in their immediate aftermath), it is not realistic to rely on the domestic police. Many police forces have typically been involved in the previous violence, as the line between police and militia forces is blurry in many internal conflicts. However, policing must be performed, especially if the parties to the conflict live in intermingled areas.

In Somalia, although there was success in the Australian section and in parts of the north, the development of local policing was neglected in most areas of the country. The problem was recognized late, and when planning was done, money was not forthcoming to carry it out. In part, the problem was due to the shortage of funds in the UN Department of Peacekeeping Operations (DPKO) which did not want to pay for police and judicial operations from its budget and, in part, the failure of member-states to volunteer sufficient and appropriate personnel. In Bosnia, an unarmed International Police Task Force (IPTF) was sent in after the Dayton Accords to monitor, advise, and train domestic police forces. But because of the relatively small numbers and limited mandate, the IPTF has had limited power to bring about substantial changes in the police forces of the entities.

The most glaring example of the international community's failure to provide for personal security was in Kosovo, where hundreds of retribution killings took place against Serbs and other minorities after the end of the air war. Although the United Nations authorized an international police force of six thousand members, it was slow in arriving and many of the personnel were not appropriate to the task. On a practical level, KFOR had to pick up what it could of the policing task, as retributions taken by the Kosovar Albanians against the remaining Serbs sullied the entire mission's reputation. However, KFOR did not possess sufficient numbers of troops or the mandate from their commanders to stop all of the reprisals.

In a broader sense, the introduction of international civilian police could be a part of a larger "justice package" to support UN missions such as has been proposed by the Australians (Plunkett 1998). Such a package would be based upon general internationally accepted principles that would provide a neutral method of achieving public order, but could be tailored for each operation in order to be accepted by the local society. The core objective of the package would be to create a functioning criminal justice system until a local one could be established. In addition to providing a neutral police force, the package could include, as appropriate, a body of criminal law and procedures based on international documents (e.g., the Universal Declaration of Human Rights, the Covenant on Civil and Political Rights, the Basic Principles of the Independence of the Judiciary) and a number of international jurists, prosecutors, defenders, and clerks (and personnel to protect them) who would not only be able to hear and process cases, but would also be charged with training their local replacements. It also could provide specialized services such as forensic science facilities (especially to produce evidence), alternative dispute mechanisms, and witness protection programs. Additionally, the package could include personnel to refurbish and manage correctional facilities and to monitor alternative sentences other than imprisonment, as well as adequate resources to fund the salaries and equipment necessary to conduct the legal process (Plunkett 1998). In addition, if necessary, the body of law could be expanded to encompass commercial law in order to foster confidence in the economy and attract foreign businesses and investors.

Lesson 5: Combatants must be disarmed and demobilized if peace is to be maintained.

Early and effective disarmament and demobilization of combatants is essential to building a durable peace (United Nations 1996). Unless this occurs, violence is very likely to recur. In Somalia during UNOSOM I and UNITAF, there was no attempt to disarm and demobilize the population. Although UNITAF recognized that disarmament was necessary to prevent resurgent violence once foreign forces departed, it steadfastly clung to its narrowly defined mandate and left the task for the follow-on UN force. However, although UNOSOM II was given the responsibility, it was not organized, equipped, or capable of accomplishing it. In Bosnia, the settlement of the internal war created a de facto partition of the country and left each ethnic group with an organized, equipped military. The presence of the NATO Stabilization Force—rather than a commitment to peace—largely deters renewed fighting. In Kosovo, the Kosovo Liberation Army (KLA) formally has been disarmed and demobilized as part of the agreed-upon principles of the cease-fire. However, if the security situation changes, the Kosovo Protection Corps, which is largely comprised of former KLA fighters, would likely constitute the base for a national army or a regenerated KLA.

Lesson 6: Most refugees and displaced persons will not—and probably should not—return to minority areas until their personal security and legal rights can be assured.

Although much of the political, economic, and social reconstruction and reconciliation necessary to provide the foundation for a stable peace cannot begin to take place until refugees and displaced persons have returned to their homes, a policing mechanism capable of ensuring their security and legal rights must be in place before large numbers will return. In Somalia, the re-settlement effort was conducted on an ad hoc basis because of the volatile security situation. While the Dayton Accords included an entire annex detailing provisions to promote and facilitate refugee and displaced person returns in Bosnia, returnees to areas in which they were a minority not only faced personal security concerns, but also many practical obstacles to impede their return. In Kosovo, a slightly different problem presented itself. With the Serb forces expelled and KFOR troops deployed to provide a security presence, many Kosovar Albanians returned more rapidly than could be accommodated by the United Nations Office of the High Commissioner for Refugees (UNHCR) relief operation set up to deal with them. Because the policing operation was slow to get under way, the Albanians committed a number of acts of retribution against the remaining Serbs with impunity.

Lesson 7: Institutional development cannot occur in the absence of an overall political agreement on the structure of the state and the provision of physical security for the citizens. However, while necessary, these conditions are not sufficient. Political will from the parties is required to consolidate them.

As the Somalia and Kosovo cases demonstrate, unless there is an overarching political agreement as to how state institutions should be structured, what powers they will have, and who will run them, institutional development cannot occur. However, even if an agreement has been signed, local parties may lack the will to implement it or seek to undermine it, as has been evident in Bosnia.

The challenge for institution builders is how to empower those who seek peace within the society and establish institutions that reward moderation and encourage compromise among contending interests (Paris 1997; Rothchild 1996). The Dayton Accords developed a loose federal arrangement with which nobody was really satisfied but met the minimum requirements of each party. The Bosnian Serbs, who were not present at the negotiations, have continually sought to weaken its powers and strengthen their control at the entity level. Since early 2000, the Bosnian Croats also have sought to undermine the Dayton structure, calling for their own state. In the absence of domestic will to institutionalize the peace settlement and to create structures capable of resolving conflicts in the future, the high representative in Bosnia has had to attempt to force ethnic political cooperation at the national level.

Lesson 8: Early elections may exacerbate conflict, legitimize hard-liners, and undermine the long-term stability of the state. However, elections cannot be delayed for too long or confidence in the system may be lost.

Although a great deal of thought was put into the development of the electoral system included in the Dayton Accords, it led to a number of unintended side effects. The initial round of elections, held only nine months after the signing of the peace agreement, reinforced and legitimized hard-liners who sought to block its implementation, both because other groups had little time to organize and because candidates only had to appeal to their ethnic group (Cousens 2001b; Eyre 2000; Sharp 1997; Woodward 1999). While numerous suggestions have been made to remedy the problems, the basic need to develop an electoral system that fosters conciliation and mediates the tension between group autonomy and national cooperation remains.

In Kosovo, the problem has been somewhat the opposite. With the international community seemingly stalled over resolving the future status of the province, the Kosovar Albanians were pushing for province-wide elections to establish a parliament and an executive capable of speaking on behalf of their community, and for managing their own internal affairs. Although the elections were finally held in November 2001, they did not provide the Kosovars with any formal power to resolve the future status of the province.

Lesson 9: Reconstructing institutions without requiring fundamental political and economic reforms will undermine long-term stability and confidence in the system.

Because a declining economy undergirded the lapse into violence in all three cases, there is general agreement by external actors that radical reforms must be undertaken in order to move from the rent-seeking, centrally planned economies of the past to ones based on the free market and liberal principles. However, as is the case with many of these lessons, this is easier said than done. In Somalia and Bosnia, political clout has been linked to the ability to provide patronage to supporters, and the economies were designed more to ensure political control than economic efficiency. Accordingly, although the entrenched leaders pay lip service to calls for reforms, they are often doing everything they can to thwart those efforts. Unless external actors begin to view Bosnia's problems more in terms of needed reforms rather than simply ensuring the short-term peace or providing aid for the reconstruction of institutions, the prospects for developing a state capable of managing conflict and promoting economic development are slim (Bildt 2001). In the absence of such reforms, there is little likelihood Bosnia will meet the conditions for entry into European institutions. In Kosovo, the international community has learned from the experiences of Bosnia and has put economic reform high on its list of priorities.

Lesson 10: Sustainable, broad-based economic development cannot occur in the absence of a national political settlement, physical security for citizens, free-market reforms, and the enforcement of a basic legal framework.

Although low levels of economic development can occur in the absence of a national political settlement, physical security, free-market reforms, and a basic legal framework, few larger businesses and investors—either foreign or domestic—will operate in an environment where their property and assets may be confiscated, ownership placed in jeopardy, and corrupt and inefficient bureaucracies may sap potential profits. None of these requisites existed (or exist today) in southern Somalia, and the economy remains heavily dependent upon subsistence agriculture. In Bosnia, although the Dayton Accords provide a national political settlement, the future of the state is still in doubt because both the Serb and Croat elements in the country seek to undermine the accords. Additionally, although physical security is provided to majority groups, the system remains riddled with corruption, deterring most economic development efforts and undermining others. In Kosovo, the absence of a national settlement deters private investors, as the question of what country's economic and legal rules will apply to business activities remains unanswered.

Lesson 11: Minority rights must be guaranteed and protected.

If the goal of the international community is to promote multiethnic states, then it must ensure that the rights of the minorities within those states be protected. Many have criticized Western governments for recognizing the secession of Slovenia and Croatia without securing guarantees for the respect of the rights and positions of the substantial minority groups within each state before independence was recognized (Galtung and Mushakoji 1999; Hagen 1999; Sharp 1997). In periods of heightened nationalist sentiments and in early stages of ethnic cleansing, minority peoples have legitimate reasons to be fearful of their own security. The increased insecurity of these groups, in turn, likely led to greater bloodshed. Additionally, it is conceivable that an agreement among the Yugoslav republics to secure minority rights would also have allowed the Kosovars to escape the worst of Milošević's excesses and averted the all-out conflict there.

If minority citizens are to render their loyalty to a state (or even a subnational government) and deem its rule legitimate, they must have confidence that their physical security as well as political, economic, and social rights will be protected. If they do not have such confidence, they will not subject themselves to that government's rule nor consider it legitimate. This is clearly the case in Bosnia, where refugees refuse to return to homes in areas in which they constitute an ethnic minority, and in Kosovo, where the Albanian population insists upon being independent of Belgrade's rule. In situations such as these, there will be no stable peace between the groups until one of three things occurs: (1) they can overcome the fear and distrust of each other, (2) they are in an entity not subject to the other's control, or (3) they are physically subjugated. While reconciliation may be possible over the longer term, it will not come quickly.

Lesson 12: The development of local governance and community structures that promote cooperation and trust among residents is imperative to long-term stability, and may be begun even in the absence of an overall national political settlement.

Although programs promoting local governance, civil society, reconciliation, and grassroots development have been around for many years, they were long treated as niceties promoted by nongovernmental organizations (NGOs) that had little impact on the real work of resolving violent conflicts. However, they are now being recognized as an integral part of the process, and military efforts often are playing a supporting role in achieving these goals. What is more, it is increasingly recognized that even if a national settlement has yet to be signed, much progress can be made at the local level that directly affects many lives.

In Somalia, UN officials were late to recognize the wisdom of promoting local and regional conciliation and governance. A number of communities, often relying on traditional conflict resolution mechanisms such as clan leaders and open forums, were able to achieve some gains, although they were not able to resolve the major feuds among rival militias. On a practical level, Somalia functioned with nothing but local and regional governments throughout the 1990s.

In Bosnia and Kosovo, the ethnic polarization has both facilitated and complicated community reconciliation efforts. On one hand, because many areas are now ethnically homogeneous, local governance and community structures have rebounded quite rapidly, allowing reconstruction and economic development to take root. However, in areas where one group is dominant but there exists a minority group, progress has been extremely slow. In attempting to make real the commitment to multiethnic societies, external actors have expended great resources trying to promote cooperation and conciliation in the Bosnian city of Brcko and the Kosovar city of Mitrovica, as well as many other communities that receive less publicity. Some have claimed external efforts will be made or broken in these two cities, arguing that if interethnic cooperation and conciliation cannot be brought about at a local level, it cannot occur at the national level (*Economist* 2000a).

Lesson 13: Some method of achieving justice for victims of abuse during the conflict must be undertaken.

Because of the high levels of violence, hatred and the desire for revenge run deep among many in Bosnia and Kosovo, and unless these feelings can be overcome they will continue to undermine a stable peace. While both Bosnia and Kosovo are covered under the International Criminal Tribunal for the former Yugoslavia (ICTY), serious shortcomings exist.

In Bosnia, the process looks good on paper, but has been impeded by a lack of cooperation by the parties and the failure to bring many of the indicted war criminals to trial. In Kosovo, the ICTY indicted Milošević and four of his top lieutenants, but has admitted it has inadequate resources to pursue wide-ranging prosecutions. In both Bosnia and Kosovo, local efforts are being explored to supplement the work of the ICTY and to attempt to hold more people accountable for their actions and improve the process of reconciliation.

In Somalia, especially in the absence of a national settlement, no attempt has been made to hold individuals accountable for past atrocities, although some local reconciliation efforts have achieved limited success.

Lesson 14: The international community must develop local ownership of the peace process if it is ultimately to be successful.

While external actors may shape and facilitate the course of activities to consolidate the peace, every statebuilding operation will be heavily dependent upon local actors. External actors may be able to create an opening and framework in which internal actors can work, but they cannot create the state in the absence of talented, willing local leaders who see it in their interest. In this sense, external actors may at times find themselves "lucky" to find a local leader who is able to bridge the divides in society and seeks to create a society that is representative and respective of all interests. At other times, however, external actors may find themselves beset with a demagogue (or demagogues) who seeks to undermine all attempts to stabilize the country. However, external actors need to remember the state that is being (re)constructed belongs to the local parties and, if peace is to be sustained and institutionalized, the process and goals must be internalized by the local parties. As such, as long as external actors are present, they must strengthen local actors committed to peace while weakening those who seek to thwart it.

In Somalia, external efforts were inadequate to allow the forces for peace to overcome the forces that had more to gain by continuing the conflict. In Bosnia, a comprehensive agreement was signed, but two of the three parties lack a commitment to it and have consistently sought to undermine portions of it they deem unfavorable to their interests. Nationalist leaders in both the Serb and Croat groups within Bosnia have sought to scapegoat the peace agreement (and the international community in general) for their populations' continued problems rather than attempt to deal with the deep and divisive issues before them. Until local actors confront each other over issues of reform, governance, and policy disputes, the process is subject to easy reversal upon the departure of the external actors. In Kosovo, local ownership will not be a problem if the final status issue is resolved in favor of independence. However, if some other outcome is decided upon, there will not only be no local ownership of the peace process, but there will be active resistance to it as well.

SUMMARY

Because internal forces are incapable of stopping the violence within their country, external actors need to develop a joint plan, as early as possible, if they seek to bring peace to that country. This plan must include a long-term holistic military, political, economic, and social strategy, and operations should be coordinated under a single international head in the country. If a military force is needed to halt the ongoing violence, a coherent national force or regional organization should conduct it, not the United Nations. Exit strategies should be based on the achievement of agreed-upon goals, not timetables.

External actors should seek to secure a comprehensive agreement by all parties to end the violence that can provide the basis for institutional and economic development. Personal security for all members of society—especially minority ones—must be ensured from the start, former combatants must be disarmed and demobilized, and a process must be developed to provide justice to those victimized by the conflict. Refugees must be repatriated and elections held within a reasonable amount of time. In the process of developing the institutions and economy, reforms must be implemented to inhibit corruption, provide for an increasing standard of living for the residents, and lay the groundwork for meeting conditions for future regional integration.

Community-based structures are important to promoting accountability and reconciliation of local residents, and jump-starting economic development. However, in order for the efforts of the external actors to ultimately achieve success, the peace process must be internalized by the local parties and sustained through the framework of rules provided for by the state.

CHAPTER 7

CONCLUSIONS AND RECOMMENDATIONS

While most of the peacekeeping/peacebuilding missions entered into over the past decade have achieved some level of success, most suffer from significant problems as well. The most obvious shortcoming is the inability to say that any mission has brought about a lasting change in the country so that the large-scale violence that prompted the international intervention in the first place will not recur when the external actors leave.

Unless this situation can be changed, the United States and other wealthy nations may well not continue to undertake or fund such missions, except in special circumstances. They already have stopped providing soldiers to support UN peacekeeping missions, whose personnel are now drawn from developing countries whose governments generally utilize such undertakings as a way to fund, train, and equip their soldiers. It is reasonably safe to say that if the United States and the wealthier states back away from supporting peacekeeping/peacebuilding missions, the internal conflicts in many areas will not be resolved in a manner acceptable to Western standards of human rights or in a way that will lay a foundation conducive to the development of democracy—if they are resolved at all.

The question underlying this study is: How can external actors more effectively bring about lasting change in societies beset by internal conflicts that can allow a stable peace to develop? The lack of attention to (re)building the state as a foundation upon which to support, link, and reinforce other elements has been a key failure. External actors must focus on (re)building a state along three dimensions: (1) it must be capable of exercising authority over its territory and providing security to its citizens, (2) it must be effective at resolving conflicts through its institutions and promoting the general welfare of its citizens, and (3) it must provide a political identity based on accepted legitimacy.

While drawing on a limited pool of case studies cannot provide fully satisfactory lessons or conclusions, they can be used to identify patterns that have occurred. In doing so, the broad tasks that need to be recognized and handled have been set out. Finding specific solutions to those tasks, along with their implementation, is the true challenge. If the foundation for the state is laid, much of the work that has been done by academics and practitioners in many specific areas (e.g., international mediation of settlements, institutional arrangements for divided societies, the development of civil society, the conduct of elections) can be linked together to form a better reinforcing structure that will be able to withstand the inevitable challenges to peace that will arise.

GENERAL CONCLUSIONS

There is a growing recognition that the challenges confronting the post-cold war international system are different than those that dominated security planners and academicians over the past fifty years. While the physical security of the major powers is not directly threatened, internal conflicts spawned by identity issues and economic interests offend humanitarian sensibilities, eat away at regional stability, and generate a number of undesirable side effects. However, because the impact of such conflicts is less direct, there is a limit to the willingness of the major powers to bear the casualties and the costs necessary to resolve them. Often prompted by the humanitarian outcry from their domestic constituents, leaders are willing to "do something" to help, as long as it can be done at a limited cost.

In the future, interventions in internal conflicts for largely humanitarian reasons will generally be multilateral undertakings in order to share the burden and secure broader legitimacy. Because of the dismal record of UN military action over the past decade, future military interventions likely will be led by a major power (with multilateral support) or a capable regional organization such as NATO. While many will seek a UN blessing for their actions, some may not if action is likely to be thwarted by a permanent member of the UN Security Council. For practical reasons, however, the peacebuilding/statebuilding missions that follow likely will be performed under a UN umbrella.

While sovereignty has become a less reflexive reason not to intervene, it is unlikely that there will be a codification of new norms or rules on when intervention should or should not occur. The major powers will resist any criteria that prevent them from taking action when they deem it in their interests or criteria that seek to "obligate" them to take action if certain conditions are met.

While the sovereign state may never have had the authority and control that many suggest it had, it is far from dead. Instead, the newer international context has altered the scope of state authority rather than generated some fundamental new way of organizing political life (Krasner 2001). Buffeted by increasing global interchange from above and increasing assertions of ethnic identity from below, leaders of states are often trapped by conflicting demands and reluctant to make agreements that cede authority, fearing that they will be undermined by domestic challengers espousing more traditional notions of sovereignty.

Although the sovereign state is not dead, statebuilders cannot—and should not—seek to rebuild the current states in crisis along the lines of early European states, hoping that they will just naturally evolve and mature into the stable democracies now found in Europe. Not only would that require a recognition that statebuilding as it occurred in Europe did not conform to presently accepted notions of human rights and that it may take many decades (if not centuries), it also fails to recognize that Europe today is moving away from that design. It also must be recognized that the international system of today will not permit it.

While the debate will continue in theoretical circles, the concept of the sovereign state must also be addressed on a practical level. A notion of layered sovereignty is needed, in which the state shares authority with entities both below and above it.

In this scenario, increased authority and autonomy would be granted to groups within the territorial confines of the state. Local governance efforts and civil society may be most effective at alleviating needs in the short term, which must occur if a peace is to take root. External actors (NGOs and international lending agencies, in particular) could work with subnational units to jump-start economic development and restore basic services such as health and education. NGOs are well suited to these tasks and have more flexibility to adapt to changing conditions and needs than can state-directed bilateral assistance programs. Smaller, more widely spread lending programs may also both reduce the incidence of corruption and weaken some of the "perquisites" of state sovereignty (as international lending in the past has typically been reserved for national governments). In this sense, external actors would be in closer contact with those who most need their services and would reduce the number of hands the assistance must pass through, getting it there faster and with less lost to corruption.

The state would provide the overall framework of rules and serve as a facilitator, coordinator, and arbitrator of the subnational entities. Outside of handling security needs and a common legal framework based on the rule of law, developing national institutions and economic development strategies (including basic infrastructure needs), and serving as a political identity, most other aspects of governance would be handled at the subnational or regional levels. This "leaner" state would be less susceptible to corruption (since less money would be passing through it), less likely to be recentralized under authoritarian rule, and would be more accountable to subnational bodies because of their increased powers.

On a regional level, economic and social associations could be formed. On the economic front, joint policies could be developed to expand markets, harmonize labor and tariff provisions, and attract foreign investment. Social associations could be promoted to allow ethnic groups that straddle borders to form ties that can promote cultural identities and provide pressure on governments to respect minority rights.

While this form of layered sovereignty will not solve all of the problems that confront a state emerging from a brutal conflict, it will allow many of the most pressing concerns to be dealt with in a way that addresses the minimal needs of both the internal and external actors. It also has the advantage of allowing the different ethnic groups greater security and control over their own affairs, while providing greater economic opportunity to all.

While a state that is capable, effective, and legitimate embedded in a system of layered sovereignty could, in theory, host a number of different forms of governments, democracy has proven to be the most successful form that has been tried. In addition to pulling in a variety of viewpoints into the policy development process, democracy enables citizens to constrain their leaders through horizontal (legislative and judicial constraints) and vertical (the electoral process) accountability mechanisms and to channel conflicts through established procedures and institutions. Authoritarian systems may be capable, effective, and even legitimate; however, there are no institutionalized procedures for citizens to hold their leaders accountable if they fail in any or all of the dimensions laid out.

While the conflicts in each of the three case studies had elements of ethnic strife, the real roots lay in the quest for power and/or economic advantage. However, because leaders rallied people around ethnic banners to secure support and prompted violence along those lines, the conflicts, for practical purposes, became ethnic conflicts. Thus, polarized and divided societies were left in the wake of the conflicts.

POLICY RECOMMENDATIONS

Although lessons have been accumulating from the peacebuilding operations of the past decade, there has yet to be developed a comprehensive plan that details what tasks need to be done and how to go about doing them that could provide a basis for future operations. While the United Nations may or may not be the appropriate organization to do so, no country has stepped forward with one either. President Clinton authorized national political-military contingency planning for hot spots in Presidential Decision Directive 56 (PDD-56) in 1997, but the focus was narrow. Because President George W. Bush's advisors have sought to draw down U.S. troops committed to the ongoing peace operations in Bosnia and Kosovo and have indicated that the new administration is unlikely to support peacebuilding operations in the future, contingency planning is unlikely to occur.

However, it is likely that President Bush and other leaders in the West will be drawn into such operations in the future, as the chairman of the joint chiefs of staff has acknowledged (AP 2000). The failure to prepare a plan all but certainly condemns future operations to the hodgepodge, stopgap, wishful-thinking actions by the international community that have yet to succeed in bringing about a stable peace.

Devising a comprehensive, general plan that can be modified to fit specific peacebuilding operations should be a priority if we are to move beyond the limited successes we have had to date (Snow 2000). The core of that plan should be premised on creating a state that is capable of exercising authority over its territory and providing security to its citizens, is effective at resolving conflicts through its institutions and promoting the general welfare of its citizens, and serves as a political identity based on legitimacy. The numerous other tasks that need to be accomplished to consolidate peace would then be set upon that basic state foundation.

There is no doubt that it will be difficult to reach a consensus on such a plan, but even the development of competing plans would provide a more workable arrangement than currently exists. Even more useful could be international simulations—or what Donald Snow (2000) calls "peace games" (analogous to the more familiar "war games")—in which scenarios are developed, procedures are practiced, and concepts refined as participants learn to work with each other across international and institutional boundaries and cultures. This type of planning and preparing would inevitably result in a more holistic and realistic approach to peacebuilding, recognizing that efforts to achieve security, reform institutions, promote economic development, and bring about social reconciliation must be pursued in a more complementary and integrated manner.

Early warning of humanitarian emergencies rarely is a problem, but government agencies are often overburdened as limited resources are generally directed at the parts of the world in which such crises are likely to occur. However, there are tremendous resources and expertise on these areas in the academic community, think tanks, and NGOs that could be better harnessed to support decision makers. Quasi-official working groups could be established on such hot spots that are able to modify a general peacebuilding plan to the specific needs of the country in conflict, taking into account its history, cultural factors, and other special circumstances.

In relation to the three dimensions of the state, a number of policy recommendations can be identified.

Authority and Security

As set out in general lessons in chapter 6, the United Nations has proved incapable of successfully exercising military force. If force needs to be applied, it should be left to a coherent nationally led force or a competent regional organ such as NATO. However, while such forces have proved successful at stopping large-scale violence, it is clear that they still have experienced significant shortcomings. Units taking part in such operations should be designated and trained in advance in the skills needed to perform peacekeeping effectively in order to reduce casualties on all sides. Specialized training in urban warfare, policing, and negotiating specifically are needed.

In general, peacebuilding missions have done a poor job at stopping smaller-scale violence. Part of this failure has been due to a hesitancy of military leadership to take on the mission, and part is due to not having the civilian police forces in sufficient numbers deployed quickly enough. This is a relatively easy problem to fix. The recent Report of the Panel on United Nations Peace Operations (the "Brahimi" report) called on the United Nations to create a ready reserve force of civilian police deployable on short notice. The European Union also announced plans in 2000 to set up a five-thousand-person force of specially trained police officers to respond more rapidly to future international crises.

The basis for such a plan is straightforward. A robust (in numbers and equipment) civilian police force that can be deployed within days after military forces have secured an area should be readied before an intervention is undertaken. An international team of judges, lawyers, and clerks that could implement the rule of law early in the peacebuilding effort should soon follow this force. While such a police force would not be capable of handling major threats to peace, the military could be held in reserve, providing reinforcements as necessary. This police force could gradually assume a greater burden for public security, and in the process, train a domestic force to take on law enforcement responsibilities as they are able. In most cases, a robust policing effort could prevent large numbers of military forces from getting bogged down in peacekeeping missions (and may allow for an easier—and earlier—decision to be made to initiate peacebuilding activities).

The United Nations has done considerable work in the field of disarmament, demobilization, and reintegration and has standard plans available. However, disarmament of unwilling combatants must be done by a well-armed, capable military force; it cannot be done by unarmed or lightly armed UN peacekeepers unless the program is voluntary. Ideally, planning specific to the country in question should take place in advance of an intervention (such as where to organize demobilization camps; where to store weapons; how to secure needed supplies such as food, water, shelter; and other assorted issues), and many of these decisions must be made in tandem with the intervening military force. Again, while some of these decisions must wait until a cease-fire has been achieved, much of the basic planning can and should be done in advance of the intervention.

Institutional and Economic Development

Once physical security is provided, external actors can do a number of things to support the establishment of institutions and promote economic development. In helping states to become more effective, external actors can draw upon the extensive work that has been done (and results of actual experiences) on the benefits of different types of institutional arrangements and electoral systems for divided societies. While the specifics will need to be determined by the country in conflict, it is likely that a federal—or even confederal—system carving the subnational units along natural lines and incorporating some type of consociational arrangement at the national level to guarantee minority groups an essential veto over items they consider vital may be appropriate. Many have also suggested that a parliamentary system based on national proportional representation may help achieve more accountability over the chief executive and provide a voice to smaller groups (Diamond 1996; Hartzell 1999; Linz 1990; Linz and Stepan 1996; Sisk 1996).

In the early stages of a peacebuilding operation, one of the areas over which external actors may have the most influence is in pushing economic reforms. It is clear that simply focusing on short-term peace arrangements and the reconstruction of existing institutions will doom external efforts to failure (Bildt 1999). Using the leverage of international financial aid, donors can insist that basic reforms be made to move the economic system toward the free-market and that policies are developed to protect property rights, make markets more competitive, encourage small businesses, and inhibit institutions from lapsing into the rent-seeking behavior that reinforces nationalist leaders and benefits politically connected sectors of the economy. However, external actors must recognize that there is bound to be resistance to these efforts by previously privileged groups because their access to resources—and hence power—is curtailed.

It is clear that peace will not be consolidated unless economic development is achieved and people are given hope of a future beyond that of grinding poverty. In the southeastern European case studies, there are advantages that can be drawn upon to help secure peace that are not available to those in Africa or other regions of the world.

Although international economic assistance measures are not working as effectively as they could, substantially more financial resources have been committed to Bosnia and Kosovo than to Somalia. Additionally, phased integration schemes can be developed that tie progress in Bosnia and Kosovo

into existing European structures. For example, the entire southeastern region could begin with a Free Trade Area (modeled on the European Free
Trade Association), move to a customs union (similar to EU arrangements
with Greece and Turkey), and eventually toward accession into the EU as
countries are able to meet the necessary requirements (Steil and Woodward
1999). While this would take place over a period of years, the scheme would
provide a series of stepping-stones with rewards along the way. Another far-
reaching suggestion that has been made is to adopt the Euro as the currency
in both Bosnia and Kosovo as a way to achieve the fiscal discipline and
macroeconomic stability necessary to attract foreign investors (Steil and
Woodward 1999). Although the two entities would need to implement a
number of reforms over a period of years to do so effectively, much trade is
currently done in deutsche marks.

While linking southeastern Europe into mainstream European institutions
can be done on the basis of sound economic policies, it also must be recognized that it has important foreign and security implications as well. Surely
pro-Western, reformist governments in the southeastern region better serve
European interests than would the nationalist, authoritarian, crime-ridden
ones that would likely take over if the economies fail. While it is naïve to
think that sound fiscal policies and free trade alone will solve the problems
in the Balkans, they are essential in raising living standards and undermining nationalist leaders who exploit the poor conditions. Until this happens,
the broader political issues of borders, sovereignty, and minority rights will
remain unsolved.

In Africa, serious economic reforms are also needed, but the solutions are
different. The reality is that sub-Saharan Africa is less important to Western
economic and security interests than the Balkans and will thus suffer from
less attention and resources. While the U.S. African Growth and Opportunity Act signed into law in May 2000 provides preferential access for certain
goods exported to the U.S. market and provides incentives for private investment in Africa, it does little fundamentally to alter the plight of most
African economies.

Lacking skills, education, resources, infrastructure, and basic physical security, people in Somalia do not have a long-term perspective allowing for
the patient development of wealth. While external actors can help alleviate
many of these deficiencies with a large commitment of force, money, and
time, economic progress will remain slow for many years because the problems are so deep.

Identity Based on Legitimacy

External actors cannot create or bestow a legitimate state upon societies
in conflict. However, they can help create conditions under which legitimacy
can be fostered. Because people are often alienated from national govern-

ments, many recent efforts have focused on directly providing assistance to the local and community levels. In this environment, external actors can help develop and fund structures that pull in diverse sectors of society so that their voices can be heard and rights protected. External actors also can develop and fund programs that meet specific health, education, small business, and other community needs. For example, U.S.-led KFOR forces used $275,000 in medical equipment and supplies to entice Serb and Albanian doctors to work together in a hospital in Gnjilane while KFOR and local police provided protection (Kitfield 2000).

While these efforts require a more detailed, nuanced knowledge of the recipient society and the flexibility to adapt programs to changing local conditions (which many foreign governments do not have), many international NGOs thrive in such an environment. Although these efforts are unlikely to bring about large-scale change at the national level, they provide a substantial service to those communities that they serve.

Although efforts targeting civil society widely have become accepted as part of a peacebuilding strategy—and development strategies in general—initiatives should be expanded to include groups not normally included in such programs. While some peasant groups and village associations are included, churches and other religious organizations should be pulled into the process, as should tribal associations and clan/ethnic-based groups. Business and labor groups should also be tapped. While care needs to be taken not to show favoritism to one group over others, the point of such strategy is to engage as many people as possible through leveraging the preexisting groups that already deal with important societal needs. By engaging each other and developing a common strategy to solve community problems, people learn far more about democracy than they do from abstract democracy programs such as the United States has supported over the past two decades (Carothers 1999).

CONCLUSIONS

How well have external actors done at statebuilding? Not well enough. Many of the necessary tasks have been attempted to an extent, but insufficient priority has been placed upon establishing the state as a capable, effective, and legitimate entity. While this is only a portion of the entire peacebuilding operation, it provides a necessary foundation upon which to structure other activities.

The case studies presented here do not prove or disprove much about the ability of external actors to bring peace to a war-torn society, but serve to show past shortcomings in pursuing that objective. It should be obvious from these discussions that bringing peace to a society coming out of a brutal conflict is a difficult, long-term task, subject to bumps along the road, and is not one that can be done according to an externally imposed schedule.

If external actors are to accomplish more in the future, there are three basic things that should be done before a mission is undertaken. First, there should be a plan detailing what needs to be done to create a stable peace in that society. This study has sought to argue that the foundation of that plan needs to be focused on (re)constructing a state that (1) is capable of exercising authority over its territory and providing security to its citizens, (2) is able to effectively resolve conflicts through its institutions and promote the general welfare of its citizens, and (3) is able to serve as a political identity based on legitimacy. While the ten questions examined in each of the cases may be good starting points, much greater elaboration needs to be made on each of the tasks. For example, one cannot just say combatants must be disarmed and demobilized or that economic development must get under way. Each task must include a list of the numerous subtasks, identify who would perform them, and specify sources of funding to carry them out.

Second, there should be a consensus (domestic and international) on whether to undertake the mission and how to do it. This must be based on an honest appraisal of what needs to be done and the prospects for success, rather than rely on a "best case scenario" as is often presented to the UN Security Council and foreign governments (Brahimi 2000; Snow 2000). As early international actions in all three cases attest, limited, uncoordinated actions by external actors are unlikely to bring about the desired changes in the target society. Internal actors who have a vested interest in the current state of affairs will seek to thwart, dilute, and delay actions in the hope that external actors will go away, thinking the goal is not worth the effort.

Third, if it is decided that an operation should be undertaken, there should be a commitment of forces, finances, and political will to do what needs to be done. Too often in the past, there was great publicity when a resolution was adopted by the UN Security Council only to find that the member states were hesitant and slow to commit the resources to accomplish the mandate. If a mission is to be undertaken, external actors must commit themselves to its goals and to stick with them in the face of setbacks along the way. However, by committing themselves, they are likely to find that there are fewer casualties, greater compliance on the part of the local parties, increased success in meeting objectives, and a likelihood that the military forces committed can be withdrawn at an earlier date than if activities are done in a halfhearted manner.

The goal of this study has been to help understand what external actors can and should be doing to help move a society in conflict toward a stable peace. It should be clear from the preceding discussion that, while external actors cannot do everything that is necessary to bring about a stable peace in the wake of an internal conflict, they can do much to facilitate that end. In quelling the violence and laying the foundation for rebuilding the state, external actors are able to create an opening for peace that local actors generally cannot bring about by themselves. In this sense, external actions may not provide sufficient conditions for peace, but they often are necessary ones. If these necessary conditions are not brought about, it is highly unlikely that a state will be developed that is capable of exercising its authority over its territory and providing security to its citizens, that is able to effectively resolve conflicts through its institutions and promote general welfare of its citizens, and that is able to serve as a political identity based on accepted legitimacy. If such a state is not developed, stable peace—especially that buttressed by democracy—may be many years in coming, if it is to come at all.

References

Africa Watch. 1995. "Somalia Faces the Future: Human Rights in a Fragmented Society." New York: Africa Watch. April.

Amnesty International. 2000. "Waiting on the Doorstep: Minority Returns to Eastern Srpska." July 11.

Annan, Kofi. 1999. "Two Concepts of Sovereignty." *The Economist*. September 18.

AP (Associated Press). 2000. "Shelton: Peacekeeping Missions Unavoidable." *Washington Post*. November 17.

Ayoob, Mohammed. 1996. "State Making, State Breaking, and State Failure." In *Managing Global Chaos: Sources and Responses to International Conflict.* Edited by Chester A. Crocker and Fen Osler Hampson with Pamela Aall. Washington, DC: United States Institute of Peace Press.

Bair, Andy, and Michael J. Dziedzic. 1998. "The International Police Task Force." In *Lessons from Bosnia: The IFOR Experience*. Edited by Larry Wentz. U.S. Army: Center for Army Lessons Learned. Available at http://call.army.mil/products.

Ball, Nicole. 1996. "The Challenge of Rebuilding War-Torn Societies." In *Managing Global Chaos: Sources and Responses to International Conflict*. Edited by Chester A. Crocker and Fen Osler Hampson with Pamela Aall. Washington, DC: United States Institute of Peace Press.

Barber, Benjamin R. 1992. "Jihad vs. McWorld." *Atlantic Monthly*. March.

Betts, Richard. 1994. "The Delusion of Impartial Intervention." *Foreign Affairs* 73 (6): 20–33.

Bildt, Carl. 1999. "Throwing Away Aid in the Balkans." *NPQ: New Perspective Quarterly* 16 (5): 22–23.

———. 2001. "A Second Chance in the Balkans." *Foreign Affairs* 80 (1): 148–59.

Boutros-Ghali, Boutros. 1992a. *An Agenda for Peace: Preventative Diplomacy,*

Peacemaking, and Peacekeeping. A report of the secretary-general pursuant to the statement adopted by the Summit Meeting of the United Nations Security Council on January 31, 1992. Available at www.un.org/Docs/SG/agpeace.html.

———. 1992b. Remarks at the UN Security Council, July 23, 1992. *Facts on File 52* (2700): 623. Available at www.un.org.

———. 1992c. *The Situation in Somalia, Report of the Secretary-General,* S/24480. August 24. Available at www.un.org.

———. 1994. *Further Report of the Secretary-General Submitted in Pursuance of Resolution 866 (1993), Reviewing Options for the Future Mandate of UNOSOM II,* S/1994/12. Available at www.un.org.

———. 1997. *Report from the High Representative for Implementation of the Peace Agreement in Bosnia and Herzegovina to the Secretary-General,* S/1997/542. July 11. Available at www.un.org.

Brahimi, Lakhdar. 2000. *Report of the Panel on United Nations Peace Operations,* A/55/305–S/2000/809. Available at www.un.org/peace/reports.

Brown, Michael. 1997. "The Causes of Internal Conflict: An Overview." In *Nationalism and Ethnic Conflict.* Cambridge, MA: MIT Press.

Bugjski, Janusz. 2000. "Balkan In Dependence." *Washington Quarterly* 23 (4): 177—193.

Carothers, Thomas. 1999. *Aiding Democracy Abroad: The Learning Curve.* Washington, DC: Carnegie Endowment for International Peace.

Cassanelli, Lee V. 1997. "Somali Land Resource Issues in Historical Perspective." In *Learning from Somalia: The Lessons of Armed Humanitarian Intervention.* Edited by Walter Clarke and Jeffrey Herbst. Boulder, CO: Westview Press.

Cerny, Philip G. 1995. "Globalization and the Changing Logic of Collective Action." *International Organization* 49: 595–625.

Clarke, Walter. 1993. "Testing the World's Resolve in Somalia." *Parameters* 23 (4).

———. 1997. "Failed Visions and Uncertain Mandates in Somalia." In *Learning from Somalia: The Lessons of Armed Humanitarian Intervention.* Edited by Walter Clarke and Jeffrey Herbst. Boulder, CO: Westview Press.

Clarke, Walter, and Jeffrey Herbst. 1997. "Somalia and the Future of Humanitarian Intervention." In *Learning from Somalia: The Lessons of Armed Humanitarian Intervention.* Edited by Walter Clarke and Jeffrey Herbst. Boulder, CO: Westview Press.

Collier, Paul. 2000. "Doing Well Out of War." In *Greed and Grievance: Economic Agendas in Civil Wars.* Edited by Mats Berdal and David M. Malone. Boulder, CO: Lynne Rienner Publishers.

Connor, Walker. 1990. "When Is a Nation?" In *Ethnic and Racial Studies* 13 (1): 92–100.

Cortright, David. 1997. "Incentive Strategies for Preventing Conflict." In *The Price of Peace: Incentives and International Conflict Prevention.* Edited by David Cortright. Lanham MD: Rowman and Littlefield Publishers, Inc.

Cousens, Elizabeth M. 2001a. "Introduction." In *Peacebuilding as Politics: Cultivating Peace in Fragile Societies.* Edited by Elizabeth Cousens and Chetan Kumar with Karis Wermester. Boulder, CO: Lynne Rienner Publishers.

———. 2001b. "Building Peace in Bosnia." In *Peacebuilding as Politics: Cultivating Peace in Fragile Societies.* Edited by Elizabeth Cousens and Chetan Kumar with Karis Wermester. Boulder, CO: Lynne Rienner Publishers.

Crocker, Chester A. 1995. "The Lessons of Somalia: Not Everything Went Wrong." *Foreign Affairs* 74 (3): 2–9.

Daalder, Ivo H. 1996. "Fear and Loathing in the Former Yugoslavia." In *The International Dimensions of Internal Conflict*. Edited by Michael Brown. Cambridge, MA: MIT Press.

———. 1997. "Three Choices in Bosnia," *Washington Post*. July 18.

Daalder, Ivo H., and Michael B. G. Froman. 1999. "Dayton's Incomplete Peace: A Four-Year Checkup." *Foreign Affairs* 78 (6): 106–13.

Daalder, Ivo H., and Michael O'Hanlon. 2000. "The United States in the Balkans: There to Stay." *Washington Quarterly* 23 (4): 157–70.

Dahl, Robert, ed. 1966. *Political Oppositions in Western Democracies*. New Haven, CT: Yale University Press.

———. 1989. *Democracy and Its Critics*. New Haven, CT: Yale University Press.

Daniel, Donald C. F., and Bradd C. Hayes. 1999. "Somalia." In *Coercive Inducement and the Containment of International Crises*. Edited by Donald C. F. Daniel and Bradd C. Hayes with Chantal de Jonge Oudraat. Washington, DC: United States Institute of Peace Press.

DeFigueiredo, Rui, and Barry Weingast. 1999. "The Rationality of Fear: Political Opportunism and Ethnic Conflict." In *Civil Wars, Insecurity, and Intervention*. Edited by Barbara Walter and Jack Snyder. New York: Columbia University Press.

Deng, Francis M. 2000. "Reconciling Sovereignty with Responsibility: A Basis for International Humanitarian Action." In *Africa in World Politics: The African State System in Flux*. Edited by John Harbeson and Donald Rothchild. Boulder, CO: Westview Press.

De Soysa, Indra. 2000. "The Resource Curse: Are Civil Wars Driven by Rapacity or Paucity." In *Greed and Grievance: Economic Agendas in Civil Wars*. Edited by Mats Berdal and David M. Malone. Boulder, CO: Lynne Rienner Publishers.

Diamond, Larry. 1996. "Democracy in Latin America: Degrees, Illusions, and Directions for Consolidation." In *Beyond Sovereignty: Collectively Defending Democracy in the Americas*. Edited by Tom Farer. Baltimore, MD: Johns Hopkins University Press.

Doyle, Michael W., and Nicholas Sambanis. 2000. "International Peacebuilding: A Theoretical and Quantitative Analysis." *American Political Science Review* 94: 779–801.

Drysdale, John. 1997. "Foreign Military Intervention in Somalia: The Root Cause of the Shift from UN Peacekeeping to Peacemaking and its Consequences." In *Learning from Somalia: The Lessons of Armed Humanitarian Intervention*. Edited by Walter Clarke and Jeffrey Herbst. Boulder, CO: Westview Press.

Duffield, Mark. 2000. "Globalization, Transborder Trade, and War Economies." In *Greed and Grievance: Economic Agendas in Civil Wars*. Edited by Mats Berdal and David M. Malone. Boulder, CO: Lynne Rienner Publishers.

Economist. 2000a. "Reconstructing Kosovo." March 18.

———. 2000b. "Hard Men Win." November 18.

Erlanger, Steven. 2000. "U.N. Official Warns of Losing the Peace in Kosovo." *New York Times on the Web*. July 3.

———. 2001. "In Farewell to Kosovo, U.N. Aide Urges Elections." *New York Times on the Web*. January 14.

Eyre, Dana P. 2000. "Clueless in Sarajevo." *Peace Review* 12 (1): 111–16.

Foley, Michael W., and Bob Edwards. 1996. "The Paradox of Civil Society." *Journal of Democracy* 7 (3): 38–52.

Gaddis, John Lewis. 1994. "Toward the Post-Cold War World." In *The Future of American Foreign Policy*. 2d ed. Edited by Eugene Wittkopf. New York: St. Martin's Press.

Gall, Carlotta. 2000. "U.N. Mission in Kosovo Proposes to Set Up a War Crimes Court." *New York Times on the Web*. June 23.

———. 2001. "U.N. Officials Revive Plan to Return Serbian Refugees to Kosovo." *New York Times on the Web*. June 8.

Galtung, Johan, and Kinhide Mushakoji. 1999. "The Crisis In and Around Kosovo/a: The Transcend Perspective." *Social Alternatives* 18 (3): 72–74.

Ganzglass, Martin R. 1997. "The Restoration of the Somali Justice System." In *Learning From Somalia: The Lessons of Armed Humanitarian Intervention*. Edited by Walter Clarke and Jeffrey Herbst. Boulder, CO: Westview Press.

GAO (United States General Accounting Office). 2000. *Balkans Security: Current and Projected Factors Affecting Regional Stability*. Briefing report to the chairman, Committee on Armed Services, House of Representatives, GAO/NSIAD-00-125BR. April.

Gellner, Ernest. 1983. *Nations and Nationalism*. Oxford: Blackwell.

General Framework Agreement for Peace in Bosnia and Herzegovina. The full text of the agreement (along with annexes and appendixes) is available on several websites, including that of NATO (www.nato.int).

George, Alexander L. 1979. "Case Studies and Theory Development: The Method of Structured, Focused Comparison." In *Diplomacy: New Approaches in History, Theory, and Policy*. Edited by Paul Gordon Lauren. New York: Free Press.

Global Witness. 1998. *A Rough Trade: The Role of Companies and Governments in the Angolan Conflict*. London: Global Witness Ltd.

Greenfeld, Liah. 1997. "The Political Significance of Culture." In *The Brown Journal of World Affairs* 4: 187–95.

Gurr, Ted Robert. 1993. *Minorities at Risk: A Global View of Ethnopolitical Conflicts*. Washington, DC: United States Institute of Peace Press.

———. 1996. "Minorities, Nationalists, and Ethnopolitical Conflict." In *Managing Global Chaos: Sources and Responses to International Conflict*. Edited by Chester A. Crocker and Fen Osler Hampson with Pamela Aall. Washington, DC: United States Institute of Peace Press.

Hagen, William A. 1999. "The Balkans' Lethal Nationalisms: The Historical Roots of the Kosovo War." *Foreign Affairs* 78 (4): 52–65.

Hartzell, Caroline. 1999. "Explaining the Stability of Negotiated Settlements to Intrastate Wars." *Journal of Conflict Resolution* 43: 3–23.

Henneberger, Melinda. 2001. "Tentative Homecomings in Kosovo, without the Homes." *New York Times on the Web*. November 19.

Herbst, Jeffrey. 1996. "Responding to State Failure in Africa." *International Security* 21 (3): 120–44.

———. 2000. *States and Power in Africa: Comparative Lessons in Authority and Control*. Princeton, NJ: Princeton University Press.

Herz, John. 1950. "Idealist Internationalism and the Security Dilemma." *World Politics* 2: 157–80.

———. 1959. *International Politics in the Atomic Age*. New York: Columbia University Press.

———. 1968. "The Territorial State Revisited: Reflections on the Future of the State." *Journal of the Northeastern Political Science Association* 1: 12–34.

Hirsch, John L. 2001. *Sierra Leone: Diamonds and the Struggle for Democracy*. Boulder, CO: Lynne Rienner Publishers.

Hirsch, John L., and Robert B. Oakley. 1995. *Somalia and Operation Restore Hope: Reflections on Peacekeeping and Peacemaking*. Washington, DC: United States Institute of Peace Press.

Hobbes, Thomas. [1651] 1968. *Leviathan*. Baltimore, MD: Penguin Books.

Hobsbawm, Eric J. 1983. "Mass-Producing Traditions: Europe 1870-1914." In *The Invention of Tradition*. Edited by Eric J. Hobsbawm and Terence Ranger. Cambridge: Cambridge University Press.

Hoffman, Stanley. 1998. *World Disorders: Troubled Peace in the Post-Cold War Era*. Lanham, MD: Rowman and Littlefield Publishers

Holbrooke, Richard. 2001. "Risking a New War in the Balkans." *New York Times on the Web*. April 8.

Howe, Jonathan T. 1997. "Relations between the United States and United Nations in Dealing with Somalia." In *Learning from Somalia: The Lessons of Armed Humanitarian Intervention*. Edited by Walter Clarke and Jeffrey Herbst. Boulder, CO: Westview Press.

Huntington, Samuel P. 1993. "*The Clash of Civilizations?*" Foreign Affairs 72 (3): 22–49.

ICG (International Crisis Group). 2001a. "The Wages of Sin: Confronting Bosnia's Republika Srpksa." *ICG Balkans Report Number 118*. October 8. Available at www.crisisweb.org/projects.

———. 2001b. "Bosnia's Precarious Economy: Still Not Open for Business." *ICG Balkans Report Number 115*. August 7. Available at www.crisisweb.org/projects.

———. 2001c. "No Early Exit: NATO's Continuing Challenge in Bosnia." *ICG Balkans Report Number 110*. May 22. Available at www.crisisweb.org/projects.

———. 2002a. "A Kosovo Roadmap (I): Addressing Final Status." March 1. Available at www.crisisweb.org/projects.

———. 2002b. "A Kosovo Roadmap (II): Internal Benchmarks." March 1. Available at www.crisisweb.org/projects.

———IICK (Independent International Commission on Kosovo). 2000. *The Kosovo Report*. Oxford: Oxford University Press. Available at www.kosovocommission.org.

Jackson, Robert H. 1990. *Quasi-States: Sovereignty, International Relations and the Third World*. Cambridge, MA: Cambridge University Press.

———. 1992. "Juridical Statehood in Sub-Saharan Africa." *Journal of International Affairs* 46 (1): 1–16.

Jackson, Robert H., and Carl Rosberg. 1982. "Why Africa's Weak States Persist: The Empirical and the Juridical in Statehood." *World Politics* 35 (1): 1–24.

Jelavich, Charles, and Barbara Jelavich, eds. 1963. *The Balkans in Transition: Essays on the Development of Balkan Life and Politics Since the Eighteenth Century*. Berkeley and Los Angeles, CA: University of California Press.

Jentleson, Bruce. 2000. "Preventative Diplomacy: A Conceptual and Analytical Framework." In *Opportunities Missed, Opportunities Seized: Preventative Diplomacy in the Post-Cold War World*. Edited by Bruce Jentleson. Lanham, MD: Rowman and Littlefield Publishers.

Jounge Oudraat, Chantal de. 1999. "Bosnia." In *Coercive Inducement and the Containment of International Crises*. Edited by Donald C. F. Daniel and Bradd C. Hayes with Chantal de Jounge Oudraat. Washington, DC: United States Institute of Peace Press.

Judah, Tim. 2000. *Kosovo: War and Revenge*. New Haven, CT: Yale University Press.

Kaplan, Robert D. 1994. *Balkan Ghosts: A Journey through History*. New York: Vintage Books.

Keen, David. 2000. "Incentives and Disincentives for Violence." In *Greed and Grievance: Economic Agendas in Civil Wars*. Edited by Mats Berdal and David M. Malone. Boulder, CO: Lynne Rienner Publishers.

Kissinger, Henry. 1999. "No U.S. Ground Forces for Kosovo." *Washington Post*. February 22.

Kitfield, James. 2000. "Lessons from Kosovo and Bosnia." *National Journal*. December 23.

Kohler, Horst. 2000. "Rebuilding Business in Kosovo." On Kosovo: Prospects for Peace. CNN Interactive. Available at www.cnn.com/SPECIALS/2 . . . osovo/stories/future/. Accessed February 7, 2000.

Krasner, Stephen D. 1999. *Sovereignty: Organized Hypocrisy*. Princeton, NJ: Princeton University Press.

———. 2001. "Sovereignty." *Foreign Policy*. January/February: 20–29.

Kritz, Neil J. 1996. "The Rule of Law in the Postconflict Phase: Building a Stable Peace." In *Managing Global Chaos: Sources and Responses to International Conflict*. Edited by Chester A. Crocker and Fen Osler Hampson with Pamela Aall. Washington, DC: United States Institute of Peace Press.

Lake, David, and Donald Rothchild. 1998. "Spreading Fear: The Genesis of Transnational Ethnic Conflict." In *The International Spread of Ethnic Conflict: Fear, Diffusion, and Escalation*. Edited by David Lake and Donald Rothchild. Princeton, NJ: Princeton University Press.

Landes, David S. 1999. *The Wealth and Poverty of Nations: Why Some Are So Rich and Some So Poor*. New York: W. W. Norton.

Lapidoth, Ruth. 1996. *Autonomy: Flexible Solutions to Ethnic Conflicts*. Washington, DC: United States Institute of Peace Press.

Levi, Margaret. 1990. "A Logic of Institutional Change." In *The Limits of Rationality*. Edited by Karen Schweers Cook and Margaret Levi. Chicago: University of Chicago Press.

Lewis, I. M. 1993. "Misunderstanding Somalia." *Anthropology Today* 9 (4).

Lijphart, Arend. 1977. *Democracy in Plural Societies*. New Haven, CT: Yale University Press.

Linz, Juan J. 1990. "The Perils of Presidentialism." *Journal of Democracy* 1: 51–69.

Linz, Juan J., and Alfred Stepan. 1996. *Problems of Democratic Transition and Consolidation: Southern Europe, South America, and Post-Communist Europe*. Baltimore: Johns Hopkins University Press.

Lipset, Seymour Martin. 1994. "The Social Requisites of Democracy Revisited." *The American Sociological Review* 59: 1–22.

Locke, John. [1689] 1980. *Second Treatise on Government*. Indianapolis, IN: Hackett Publishing Company.

Madison, James. [1788] 1987. *The Federalist Papers*. Edited by Issac Kramnick. New York: Viking-Penguin.

Malcolm, Noel. 1998. *Kosovo: A Short History*. New York: New York University Press.

Mandelbaum, Michael. 1996. "Foreign Policy as Social Work." *Foreign Affairs* 74 (1): 16–33.

March, James G., and Johan P. Olson. 1998. "The Institutional Dynamics of International Political Orders." *International Organization* 52: 943–60.

Marquis, Christopher, with Carlotta Gall. 2000. "Congressional Report Says Corruption is Stifling Bosnia." *New York Times on the Web*. July 7.

Matthews, Jessica. 1997. "Power Shift." *Foreign Affairs* 76 (1): 50–66.

Menkhaus, Ken. 1997. "International Peacebuilding and the Dynamics of Local and National Reconciliation in Somalia." In *Learning from Somalia: The Lessons of Armed Humanitarian Intervention*. Edited by Walter Clarke and Jeffrey Herbst. Boulder, CO: Westview Press.

Meron, Theodor. 1997. "Answering for War Crimes." *Foreign Affairs* 76 (1): 2–8.

Mertus, Julie A. 1999. *Kosovo: How Myths and Truths Started a War*. Berkeley, CA: University of California Press.

NATO (North Atlantic Treaty Organization). 1999. "NATO's Role in Relation to the Conflict in Kosovo." July 15. Available at www.nato.int/kosovo/history.htm.

Natsios, Andrew S. 1997. "Humanitarian Relief Intervention in Somalia: The Economics of Chaos. In *Learning from Somalia: The Lessons of Armed Humanitarian Intervention*. Edited by Walter Clarke and Jeffrey Herbst. Boulder, CO: Westview Press.

North, Douglass C. 1990. *Institutions, Institutional Change and Economic Performance*. Cambridge, MA: Cambridge University Press.

Nye, Joseph S. 2000. *Understanding International Conflicts: An Introduction to Theory and History*. 3d ed. New York: Longman.

O'Donnell, Guillermo, and Philippe Schmitter. 1986. *Transitions from Authoritarian Rule: Tentative Conclusions about Uncertain Democracies*. Baltimore, MD: Johns Hopkins University Press.

Olson, Mancur. 1965. *The Logic of Collective Action*. Cambridge, MA: Harvard University Press.

———. 1996. "Big Bills Left on the Sidewalk: Why Some Nations Are Rich and Others Poor." *Journal of Economic Perspectives* 10 (2): 3–24.

Orentlicher, Diane F. 1991. "Settling Accounts: The Duty to Prosecute Human Rights Violations of a Prior Regime." *Yale Law Review* 100: 2537–615.

OSCE (Organization for Security and Cooperation in Europe) Mission in Kosovo, Department of Human Rights and Rule of Law. 2000. *Review of the Criminal Justice System*, 1 February–31 July 2000. Available at www.osce.org/kosovo/documents/reports/justice.

OSCE. 2001. "High Representative and OSCE Welcome Progress Made in Bosnia and Herzegovina, Call for More Reforms." Press Release. October 18. Available at www.osce.org/news.

OTI (Office of Transition Initiatives, Bureau of Humanitarian Responses, U.S. Agency for International Development, U.S. Department of State). 2000a.

OTI Program Summary. November 2000: Kosovo. Available at www.usaid.gov.

———. 2000b. *Results Review FY 1999: Bosnia and Herzegovina*. Available at www.usaid.gov.

Ottaway, Marina. 1999. *Africa's New Leaders: Democracy or State Reconstruction?* Washington, DC: Carnegie Endowment for International Peace.

Paris, Roland. 1997. "Peacebuilding and the Limits of Liberal Internationalism." *International Security* 22: 54–89.

Perez de Cuellar, Javier. 1991. *Report of the Secretary-General on the Work of the Organization*. New York: The United Nations.

Plunkett, Mark. 1998. "Reestablishing Law and Order in Peace Maintenance." In *The Politics of Peace Maintenance*. Edited by Jarat Chopra. Boulder, CO: Lynne Rienner Publishers.

Posen, Barry. 1993. "The Security Dilemma and Ethnic Conflict." In *Ethnic Conflict and International Security*. Edited by Michael Brown. Princeton, NJ: Princeton University Press.

———. 2000. "The War for Kosovo: Serbia's Political-Military Strategy." *International Security* 24 (4): 39–85.

Przeworski, Adam. 1991. *Democracy and the Market: Political and Economic Reforms in Eastern Europe and Latin America*. United Kingdom: Cambridge University Press.

Putnam, Robert. 1993. *Making Democracy Work: Civic Traditions in Modern Italy*. Princeton, NJ: Princeton University Press.

———. 1995. "Bowling Alone: America's Declining Social Capital." *Journal of Democracy* 6 (1): 65–78.

Renan, Ernest. [1882] 1996. "What Is a Nation?" In *Becoming National: A Reader*. Edited by Geoff Eley and Ronald Grigor Suny. New York: Oxford.

Reno, William. 1996. Paper presented at the United Nations University (Helsinki, Finland) World Institute for Development Economics Research meeting at the Queen Elizabeth House, Oxford, on "The Political Economy of Humanitarian Emergencies." October. Cited in Mark Duffield. 2000. "Globalization, Transborder Trade, and War Economies." In *Greed and Grievance: Economic Agendas in Civil Wars*. Edited by Mats Berdal and David M. Malone. Boulder, CO: Lynne Rienner Publishers.

———. 1998. *Warlord Politics and African States*. Boulder, CO: Lynne Rienner Publishers.

———. 2000a. "Africa's Weak States, Nonstate Actors, and the Privatization of Interstate Relations." In *Africa in World Politics: The African State System in Flux*. Edited by John Harbeson and Donald Rothchild. Boulder, CO: Westview Press.

———. 2000b. "Shadow States and the Political Economy of Civil Wars." In *Greed and Grievance: Economic Agendas in Civil Wars*. Edited by Mats Berdal and David M. Malone. Boulder, CO: Lynne Rienner Publishers.

Robertson, (Lord) George. 2000. "The Work Ahead in Bosnia." *New York Times on the Web*. November 25.

Rohde, David. 2000. "Kosovo Seething." *Foreign Affairs* 79 (3): 65–79.

Rosenau, James N. 1990. "The State in an Era of Cascading Politics." In *The Elusive State: International and Comparative Perspectives*. Edited by James Caporaso. London: Sage Publications.

Rothchild, Donald. 1996. "Conclusion: Responding to Africa's Post-Cold War Conflicts." In *Africa in the New International Order: Rethinking State Sovereignty and Regional Security*. Edited by Edmond J. Keller and Donald Rothchild. Boulder CO: Lynne Rienner Publishers.

Rousseau, Jean-Jacques. [1762] 1997. *Rousseau—The Social Contract and Other Later Political Writings* (Cambridge Texts in the History of Political Thought). Edited by Victor Gourevitch. New York: Cambridge University Press.

Sahnoun, Mohamed. 1994. *Somalia: Missed Opportunities*. Washington, DC: The United States Institute of Peace Press.

Schedler, Andreas. 1999. "Conceptualizing Accountability." In *The Self-Restraining State: Power and Accountability in New Democracies*. Edited by Andreas Schedler, Larry Diamond, and Marc F. Plattner. Boulder, CO: Lynne Rienner Publishers.

Sell, Louie. 2001. "Kosovo: Getting Out with Peace and Honor Intact." *Problems of Post-Communism* 48 (2): 3–14.

Sharp, Jane M. O. 1997. "Dayton Report Card." *International Security* 22 (3): 101–37.

Shearer, David. 1998. *Private Armies and Military Intervention*. London: International Institute for Strategic Studies, Adelphi Paper No. 316.

Siegal, Pascale Combelles. 1998. "Target Bosnia: Integrating Information Activities in Peace Operations." U.S. Army: Center for Army Lessons Learned. Available at http://call.army.mil/products/spc_prod/ccrp/target/tarch1/htm.

Sisk, Timothy D. 1996. *Power Sharing and International Mediation in Ethnic Conflicts*. Washington, DC: United States Institute of Peace Press.

Smith, Jeffrey. 2000. "'Racist' Newspaper Riles U.N. in Kosovo." *Washington Post*. April 3.

Smooha, Sammy, and Theodor Hanf. 1992. "The Diverse Modes of Conflict Regulation in Deeply Divided Societies." *International Journal of Comparative Sociology* 33: 26–47.

Snow, Donald M. 1996. *Uncivil Wars: International Security and the New Internal Conflicts*. Boulder, CO: Lynne Rienner Publishers.

———. 1997. *Distant Thunder: Patterns of Conflict in the Developing World*. 2d ed. Armonk, NY: M. E. Sharpe.

———. 2000. *When America Fights: The Uses of U.S. Military Force*. Washington, DC: CQ Press.

Stedman, Stephen John. 1997. "Spoiler Problems in Peace Processes." *International Security* 22 (2): 5–53.

Steil, Benn and Susan L. Woodward. 1999. "A European "New Deal" for the Balkans." *Foreign Affairs* 78 (6): 95–105.

Steiner, Jurg. 1998. *European Democracies*. 4th Edition. New York: Longman.

Stevenson, Jonathan. 1993. "Hope Restored in Somalia?" *Foreign Policy*. Summer.

Talbott, Strobe. 1999. "The Balkan Question and the European Answer." Address at the Aspen Institute, Aspen, CO. August 24.

Tilly, Charles. 1990. *Coercion, Capital, and European States, A.D. 990–1992*. Cambridge, MA: Blackwell.

———. 1992. "Prisoners of the State." *International Social Science Journal* 133: 329–42.

————, ed. 1975. *The Formation of National States in Western Europe*. Princeton, NJ: Princeton University Press.

Tyrrell, Martin. 1996. "Nation-States and States of Mind: Nationalism as Psychology." *Critical Review* 10: 233–50.

UNAUSA (United Nations Association of the United States of America). 2000. *Peacekeeping at the Brink: Recommendations for Urgent International Action on Kosovo*. February. Available at www.unausa.org.

————. 2001. *The Preparedness Gap: Making Peace Operations Work in the 21st Century*. Available at www.unausa.org.

United Nations. 1945. *Charter of the United Nations*. Available at www.un.org.

————. 1993. Press Release 37. March 23. Available at www.un.org.

————. 1996. *An Inventory of Post-Conflict Peace-Building Activities*, ST/ESA/246. New York: The United Nations.

————. 1999. "United Nations Interim Administration Mission in Kosovo: Bringing Peace to Kosovo: Mandate and Tasks." Accessed on August 18 at www.un.org/peace/kosovo/pages/kosovo12.htm.

————. 2000a. "UNMIK 1st Anniversary Backgrounder—Returns—5 June 2000." Accessed on April 7, 2001, at www.un.org/peace/kosovo.

————. 2000b. "Report of the Panel on United Nations Peace Operations." (The Brahimi Report), A/55/305–S/2000/809. Available at www.un.org/peace/reports.

————. 2001a. "What Is UNMIK?" Accessed on May 10. Available at www.un.org/peace/kosovo/pages/unmik12.html.

————. 2001b. "Report of the Security Council Mission on the Implementations of Security Council Resolution 1244 (1999)." S/2001/600. June 19.

————. 2002. "Report of the Secretary General on the United Nations Interim Mission in Kosovo." S/2002/62. January 15.

United States Department of Defense. 2000. *Report to Congress: Kosovo/Operation Allied Force After-Action Report*. January 31.

United States General Accounting Office. 2000. *Balkans Security: Current and Projected Factors Affecting Regional Stability*. Briefing Report to the Chairman, Committee on Armed Services, House of Representatives, GAO/NSIAD-00-125BR. April.

United States Mission to the United Nations. 1997. *Global Humanitarian Emergencies*. New York: United Nations Press.

USAID (United States Agency for International Development). 1999. *Kosovo: Refugee Return and Stabilization*. June 22. Available at http://kosovo.info.usaid.gov.

USIP (United States Institute of Peace). 2000a. "Transatlantic Relations in the Aftermath of Kosovo." *Special Report*. May 15. Washington, DC: United States Institute of Peace Press. Available at www.usip.org/pubs.

————. 2000b. "Truth Commissions for the Former Yugoslavia." *Peacewatch* 6 (4). June. Washington, DC: United States Institute of Peace Press. Available at www.usip.org/pubs.

————. 2000c. "Bosnia's Next Five Years: Dayton and Beyond." *Special Report*. November 3. Washington, DC: United States Institute of Peace Press. Available at www.usip.org/pubs.

Walter, Barbara F. 1997. "The Critical Barrier to Civil War Settlement." *International Organization* 51: 335–64.

Weber, Max. [1922] 1964. "The Fundamental Concepts of Sociology." In *The Theory of Social and Economic Organization*. Edited by Talcott Parsons. New York: Free Press.

———. [1922] 1968. *Economy and Society: An Outline of Interpretive Sociology*. Translated by Guenther Roth and Claus Wittich. New York: Bedminster Press.

Wentz, Larry. 1998. "Bosnia—Setting the Stage." In *Lessons from Bosnia: The IFOR Experience*. Edited by Larry Wentz. U.S. Army: Center for Army Lessons Learned. Available at http://call.army.mil/products.

West, Rebecca. 1941. *Black Lamb and Grey Falcon: A Journey through Yugoslavia*. New York: Viking.

White House. Office of the Press Secretary. 1999. "Winning the Peace in Kosovo: A Progress Report." *Fact Sheet*. November 23.

Woodward, Susan. 1995. *Balkan Tragedy: Chaos and Dissolution after the Cold War*. Washington, DC: The Brookings Institution.

———. 1997. "Bosnia." *The Brookings Review* 15 (2).

———. 1999. "Transitional Election and the Dilemmas of International Assistance to Bosnia and Herzegovina." In *Three Dimensions of Peacebuilding in Bosnia: Findings from USIP-Sponsored Research and Field Projects*. Edited by Steven M. Riskin. Washington, DC: United States Institute of Peace Press.

———. 2000. "Costly Disinterest: Missed Opportunities for Preventative Diplomacy in Croatia and Bosnia and Herzegovina." In *Opportunities Missed, Opportunities Seized: Preventative Diplomacy in the Post-Cold War World*. Edited by Bruce Jentleson. Lanham, MD: Rowman and Littlefield Publishers.

World Bank. 1998. *Post Conflict Reconstruction: The Role of the World Bank*. Washington, DC: World Bank.

Young, Crawford. 2000. "The Heritage of Colonialism." In *Africa in World Politics: The African State System in Flux*. Edited by John Harbeson and Donald Rothchild. Boulder, CO: Westview Press.

Zartman, I. William. 2000. "Inter-African Negotiations and State Renewal." In *Africa in World Politics: The African State System in Flux*. Edited by John Harbeson and Donald Rothchild. Boulder, CO: Westview Press.

Zimmerman, Warren. 1999. *Origins of a Catastrophe*. New York: Times Books.

INDEX

About the Author

KATHLEEN HILL HAWK is Assistant Professor of Political Science at The University of Alabama in Huntsville.